PUZZLE BOX

VOLUME 1

Edited by

Peter Grabarchuk *and* Serhiy Grabarchuk

Andrea Gilbert
Bram Cohen
Donald Knuth
Ed Pegg, Jr.
Erich Friedman
Harry Nelson
Helen Grabarchuk
Peter Grabarchuk
Richard Candy
Serhiy Grabarchuk
Shelly Hazard
Tanya Grabarchuk

DOVER PUBLICATIONS, INC.
Mineola, New York

Contents

Bibliographical Note

Puzzle Box, Volume 1 is a new work, first published by Dover Publications, Inc.,
in 2016. All puzzles were edited and illustrated by Serhiy and Peter Grabarchuk
except for puzzles 10, 16, 33, 40, 46, 64, 89, 99, 120, 137, 157, 173, 192,
209, 211, 237, 254, 271, and 288, which were illustrated by Andrea Gilbert. A
Foreword written by Peter Winkler has been specially prepared for this edition.

International Standard Book Number

ISBN-13: 978-0-486-81004-1
ISBN-10: 0-486-81004-6

Manufactured in the United States
81004601   2016
www.doverpublications.com

Foreword

Wow, are you ever in for a treat!

In this unique volume Peter and Serhiy Grabarchuk, of the amazing Grabarchuk family, have assembled THREE HUNDRED wonderful, original puzzles – enough to keep a reasonable person entertained for a year.

And these are not just any puzzles. Flip through the enticing pictures, and you'll see one puzzle after another that departs from the norm. Some are completely new ideas; others look familiar (say, a maze) but contain some devilish twist (e.g., no left turns). Some are harder than they look; some easier. All are beautifully presented and ingeniously devised.

The authors have generously provided a "toughness rating" (2 to 5) for each puzzle. Are you in the mood for a challenge? Pick a four- or even five-star puzzle. Need something light to think about while waiting on line? Maybe two stars will do. Of course, your mileage will vary; your special talents will let you solve some toughies immediately, while your blind spots allow easy ones to remain unsolved. Yes, solutions (again with nice pictures) are included in the back, but don't be tempted. Tape them up or (better) rip them out and stuff them into your safety-deposit box. Then scribble all over the puzzles; later you can buy a dozen new copies, give 11 to friends and keep one for posterity.

If you're scanning these words while browsing in the Puzzles & Games section of your bookstore (picking out Dover books, I bet), check out puzzle 111. Looks like a word puzzle or maybe a chess puzzle, but really it's graph-theoretic – and fiendishly clever. Or, take a look at 10, or 12, or 188, 211, 219, 251, 252, 260, 271, 281, 288, or 289...it's hard to pick favorites, they're all terrific.

What makes this collection so extraordinary is that they are originals, composed and assembled by passionate puzzle mavens (including the likes of Don Knuth, world-famous author of *The Art of Computer Programming*). Hats off to a great job by all: the result is a book you can savor. Happy puzzling!

– Peter Winkler
Professor, author of
Mathematical Puzzles: A Connoisseur's Collection
and *Mathematical Mind-Benders*.
Hanover, NH, USA

Andrea Gilbert

A software engineer and puzzle designer with a life-long interest in route-finding puzzles and logic mazes. Andrea's designs have been published in various forms, and can be explored online at clickmazes.com. Several of her puzzles were manufactured and  developed as apps. Andrea has created puzzles 10, 16, 33, 40, 46, 64, 89, 99, 120, 137, 157, 163, 173, 192, 209, 211, 224, 237, 254, 271, and 288.

Bram Cohen

A computer programmer, the author of the P2P BitTorrent protocol and the first file sharing program to use the protocol. Bram actively creates puzzles in different forms and genres,  and participates in puzzle projects. More at bramcohen.com. His puzzles are 15, 38, 57, 58, 78, 95, 105, 108, 112, 131, 139, 158, 171, 178, 183, 206, 216, 244, and 287.

Donald Knuth

A computer scientist, mathematician, and professor emeritus at Stanford University. Algorithms and their analysis are his absolute domain. His famous multi-volume work *The Art of Computer Programming* is the programmer's Bible. More at www-cs-faculty.stanford.edu/~knuth. Don will puzzle you with 5, 25, 28, 42, 49, 82, 107, 110, 130, 154, 181, 195, 217, 252, 262, and 296.

Ed Pegg, Jr.

An expert on math puzzles and recreational mathematician. He works at Wolfram MathWorld, writes for the MAA online, runs mathpuzzle.com, and collaborates on many math and puzzle projects. His puzzles are 11, 20, 39, 53, 76, 84, 94, 102, 111, 123,  134, 141, 151, 160, 168, 177, 179, 184, 193, 201, 218, 225, 233, 257, 260, 272, 273, and 283.

Erich Friedman

An Associate Professor of Mathematics and ex-Chair of the Math and Computer Science Department at Stetson University. Teaches calculus and statistics. Learn more at stetson.edu/~efriedma. Erich's puzzles are 8, 14, 18, 21, 32, 45, 47, 70, 77, 81, 92, 103, 106, 115, 121, 135, 145, 152, 159, 172, 180, 186, 199, 207, 215, 227, 235, 243, 256, 264, 269, 278, 280, 293, and 298.

Harry Nelson

A mathematician, computer programmer and expert, math editor (JRM for five years), and devoted puzzle inventor with a longtime interest in puzzles of all kinds and puzzling. In 1979 he  co-discovered the 27th Mersenne prime. Harry has created puzzles 9, 27, 35, 56, 62, 73, 97, 122, 126, 144, 165, 188, 213, 229, 231, 232, 249, 265, 276, 289, and 297.

Helen Grabarchuk

Besides looking after two children, crafting, and cooking, Helen loves to create new puzzles. Actively participates in developing puzzle apps, publishing puzzle books, and different puzzle projects. See grabarchukpuzzles.com for more. Her puzzles are 13, 22, 30, 71, 88, 98, 109, 116, 136, 143, 146, 155, 164, 169, 189, 210, 214, 230, 253, 259, 263, 266, 290, and 294.

Peter Grabarchuk

A professional puzzle game designer and product manager. Peter has published thousands of puzzles, developed apps, books, mechanical toys, and run websites. More at peterpuzzle.com. His puzzles are 2, 4, 6, 12, 31, 43, 44, 54, 55, 59, 65, 67, 91, 113, 118, 138, 148, 156, 174, 190, 196, 197, 208, 219, 236, 261, 270, 279, 282, 286, and 299.

Richard Candy

Richard's lifelong interest in puzzle solving has recently inspired him to compose puzzles himself. He also enjoys music and reading and writing short stories. He has composed puzzles 7, 19, 24, 36, 41, 52, 61, 68, 69, 80, 87, 96, 124, 133, 142, 147, 162, 204, 205, 212, 226, 245, 250, 267, 274, 284, and 291 and co-authored 110 and 217.

Serhiy Grabarchuk

A metagrobologist and professional puzzle creator. Learn and play more at his website ageofpuzzles.com. Serhiy has created puzzles 3, 29, 51, 75, 79, 86, 100, 117, 125, 132, 140, 149, 150, 161, 166, 167, 175, 182, 187, 194, 198, 220, 221, 228, 234, 240, 242, 247, 248, 251, 255, 281, 285, 292, and 295 and co-authored 7, 87, 155, 162, and 245.

Shelly Hazard

An accomplished hardware writer with a highly technical background. Actively creates original logic and word puzzles and participates in different puzzle projects. More at puzzlersparadise.com. Puzzles 26, 37, 63, 72, 74, 90, 93, 114, 127, 128, 153, 170, 185, 200, 203, 222, 223, 241, 246, 275, and 277 have been mastered by Shelly.

Tanya Grabarchuk

A professional puzzle game tester and levels creator. Participated in creating and pre-publication preparations of several thousands of puzzles in apps, books, and mechanical puzzles. For more visit grabarchukpuzzles.com. Tanya has created puzzles 1, 17, 23, 34, 48, 50, 60, 66, 83, 85, 101, 104, 119, 129, 176, 191, 202, 238, 239, 258, 268, and 300.

Introduction

This collection comprises a vast spectrum of original puzzles created by the world's most renowned mathematicians, puzzle creators, and devoted puzzle lovers.

The book you hold in your hands is a unique puzzle project embracing fantastic efforts of a dozen authors, aimed to bring to all true puzzle lovers and solvers a delicious set of brainteasers of the highest possible level. In the previous double-page spread you can read about the authors of this book. We are sure you will know many of them, and we do hope this book presents greatly their unique puzzle side.

None of the puzzles in this book have been published in the printed book format, although some of them were published electronically in *100 Matchstick Puzzles* and *103 Puzzle Quizzes* Kindle books, clickmazes.com, puzzles.com, puzzlersparadise.com, and Puzzlium.

The most interesting feature of the book is that it is not a simple compilation of particular puzzles from different authors but a fusion of puzzle work of all authors involved in the project. As a result, many puzzles uncovered their hidden facets and became brighter.

There are puzzles of seventeen different types: 3D puzzles, chess puzzles, connections, dissections, foldings, geometrical puzzles, logic problems, matchstick puzzles, mazes, moving pieces, number puzzles, put-togethers, strimko, sudoku, visual puzzles, weightings, and word puzzles.

The difficulty level of each puzzle is marked by stars, 2 to 5. The average difficulty level of puzzles is 3 stars. Generally, puzzles in the book are intended for more advanced solvers, although to solve many of them you will need just a basic knowledge. Besides, a big amount of them will require more deep skills and some special knowledge, and many of these are real puzzle nuts which can bring long hours of solving and enjoyment.

There are specific requirements to solving some puzzles.

All chess puzzles use standard chess game rules. A chessboard has a standard orientation so that whites sit south of the board and blacks sit north of the board. In some chess puzzles real colors of some pieces are to be defined, so at the start they are shown in gray.

In all matchstick puzzles you should use matchsticks as unit segments. You cannot bend, break, overlap, or cross matchsticks, and you should always use them at their full length without loose ends.

In weighting puzzles with weights balancing on rods and strings it assumes that the whole system balances when both sides of each rod have equal torque. Also, assume the rods and strings are weightless.

Please note that some puzzles may have multiple solutions, and just some of them are shown in the Solution section.

We do believe every reader and solver of this puzzle collection will find many delicious puzzles to solve, and will enjoy them as much as the authors enjoyed creating and evolving them to their final shape.

– Serhiy and Peter Grabarchuk
San Jose, CA, USA

Puzzles

1 ★★☆☆☆

Divide the shape into five identical parts, cutting along the lines of the grid. Parts may be rotated or reflected.

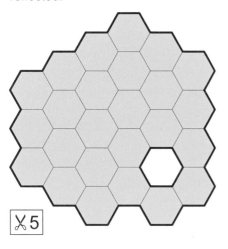

✂5

2 ★★☆☆☆

Following the lines of the grid, connect each pair of identical symbols with a single continuous line. Lines should cover all nodes of the shape, and cannot cross each other.

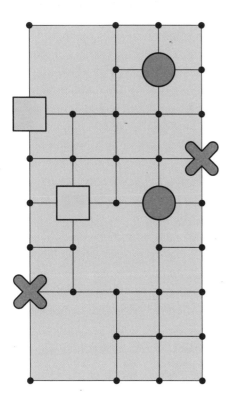

3 ★★★☆☆

Among the two dozen tangled hearts, find four pairs of interlinked ones.

4 ★★★☆☆

Fill in the grid so that each row, column, and region contains different digits 1 through 8.

1
2
3
4
5
6
7
8

		5		
	4		1	
			7	
	2			4
3		5		1
		3		
			5	
		2	6	

5 ★★★☆☆

For each of these six elements find another element which has no letter in common with its counterpart. Each answer is unique.

ALUMINUM	
ARSENIC	
HYDROGEN	
IODINE	
IRON	
NICKEL	

6 ★★★☆☆

Which pattern A through E, when folded along the dotted lines, creates the same cube as the first pattern does?

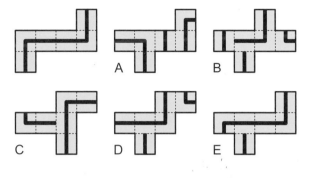

9 ★★★☆☆

Put into each empty box a digit such that all the eight indicated equations, across and down, are true. One box already contains a digit.

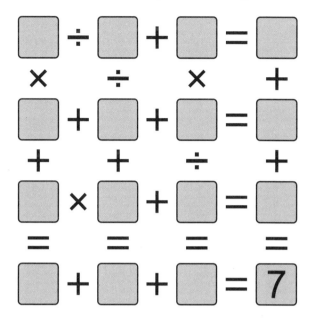

7 ★★☆☆☆

Fit the eight pieces into the grid so that pieces of the same color do not touch each other even at a corner. You can rotate pieces and mirror them, but not overlap.

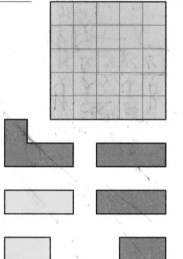

10 ★★☆☆☆

Solve the maze using just the white paths and making left turns only. Right turns are strictly forbidden, even if there is no other choice.

8 ★★☆☆☆

Label each weight in the top row with a different weight from 1 to 9, and then use those same weights in the same order in the bottom row, so that both rods balance with equal torque.

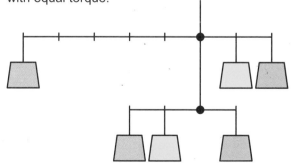

11 ★★☆☆☆

Al, Bee, Cal, Dot, and Ed all bought items from the store. Al and Bee paid 150 coins, Bee and Cal paid 200 coins, Cal and Dot paid 170 coins, Dot and Ed paid 210 coins, and Ed and Al paid 100 coins. How much did each person spend?

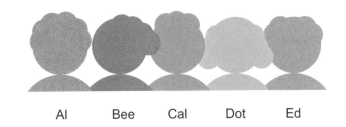

Al   Bee   Cal   Dot   Ed

12 ★★☆☆☆

Puzzle 1: How many different dancers can you spot?
   Puzzle 2: Which dancer can you spot just once?
   Puzzle 3: Which dancer can you spot three times?

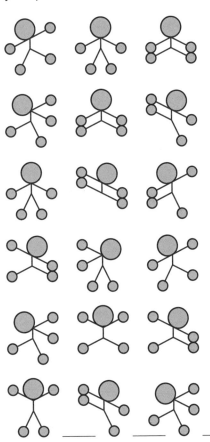

13 ★★☆☆☆

Rotate the four joined circles around the center so that all the letters form a famous 6-word proverb. Each word should read from the biggest circle to the center.

Use the table for the solution.

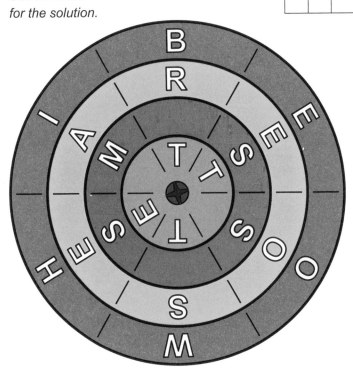

14 ★★☆☆☆

Arrange the pieces of 577 to make some shape, and then make the same shape using the pieces of 11111. You can rotate pieces, but not flip them or overlap them.

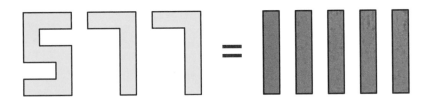

15 ★★☆☆☆

Divide the shape into two identical parts, cutting along the lines of the grid. Parts may be rotated or reflected.

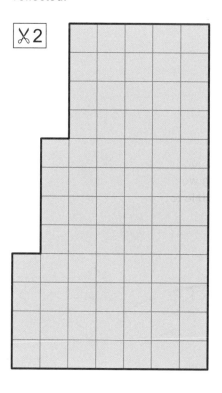

16 ★★★☆☆

Enter the maze at the bottom, stepping over the red line, then step over a blue line, then a yellow line. Repeat the sequence (red, blue, yellow, red, blue, yellow...) until you can exit over the yellow line at the top. You must finish exactly red, blue, yellow.

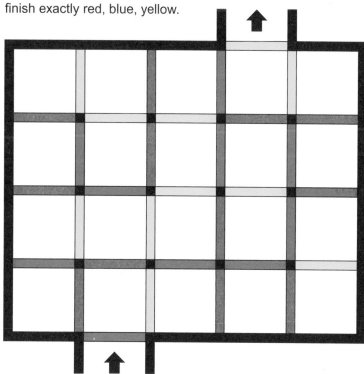

17 ★★☆☆☆

Fill in the grid so that each row, column, and stream contains different digits 1 through 5.

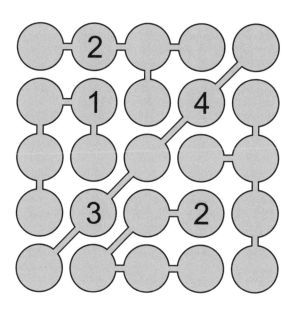

18 ★★★☆☆

Connect the dots in a loop so that each line segment has different length. The loop can cross, but will never retrace its steps, and will never pass through a point twice.

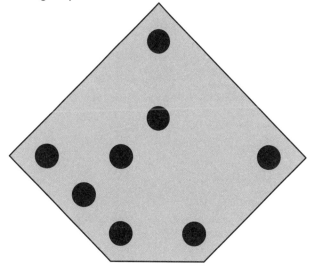

19 ★★☆☆☆

Arrange the six checkered pieces into the checkered board shown in the middle. You can rotate pieces and mirror them, but not overlap.

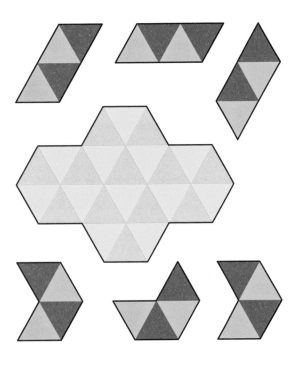

20 ★★☆☆☆

Arrange the numbers 1 to 9 in the boxes below so that each line of three boxes sums to 14. Three numbers have already been placed.

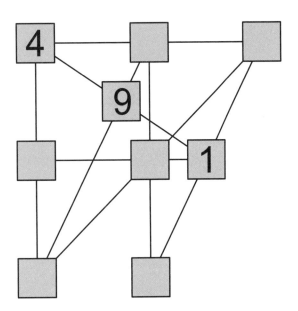

21 ★★★★☆

Draw a path to visit all of the yellow hexes exactly once. The path can start anywhere and it can change direction only when it hits the edge of the grid, itself, or one of the black hexes.

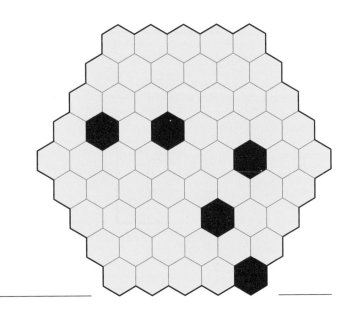

22 ★★★☆☆

One word is written in light on the dark tiles, while the other is in dark on the light ones. Then each light letter on the dark tiles was overlapped with the dark letter from the light tile immediately below it. And vice versa—each dark letter on the light tiles was overlapped with the light letter from the dark tile immediately above it. Reveal these two words—their meanings are related.

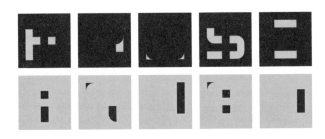

The shapes of the letters are shown below.

12

23 ★★★☆☆

Fill in the grid so that each row, column, and region contains different digits 1 through 7.

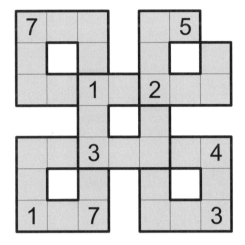

24 ★★☆☆☆

Spell the word KNIGHT letter by letter, each time jumping by means of the chess knight's move.

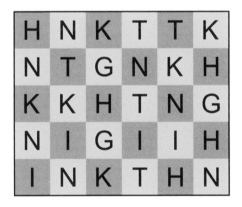

25 ★★☆☆☆

Replace the letters with the digits to get the correct calculation. The same letters in this calculation mean the same digit.

```
  N O R T H
+ S O U T H
+   E A S T
+ W E S T
─────────────
S T R E E T
```

26 ★★★☆☆

Four friends participated in July's day camp program this summer. Their parents would drop them off at the lakefront each morning and pick them up at suppertime each evening. The morning activity was a water sport of their choice and then the afternoon activity was a different non-water sport of their choice. As it happened, the friends all chose different activities during the day, though they still saw each other during lunch. Determine the full name of each friend, the water sport each chose to participate in, and the afternoon activity each chose.

   1. Mike loved kayaking. The friend whose last name was Heart loved tennis.

   2. Harry didn't play tennis. Sara didn't like archery. Ms. White didn't swim.

   3. Mr. Mann didn't participate in the pottery class.

   4. The person who went canoeing also participated in the painting session.

   5. Mike didn't play tennis. Harry's last name wasn't Smith.

   6. Sara, whose last name wasn't White, loved to sail.

	Heart	Mann	Smith	White	canoeing	kayaking	sailing	swimming	archery	painting	pottery	tennis
Cindy												
Harry												
Mike												
Sara												
archery												
painting												
pottery												
tennis												
canoeing												
kayaking												
sailing												
swimming												

Use the grid for help.

Use the table for the solution.

First Name	Last Name	Water Sport	Afternoon Activity

27 ★★★☆☆

In this chess puzzle, you are given only a list of all of the legal moves from a position. The problem is to find the current board position from which these moves arise. The notation for the moves is pretty standard. Each position can be reached by legal play starting from the usual opening position. White has four men, black has two. The legal moves are:

1. Ng4, 2. Ne4, 3. Nh3+, 4. Nd3, 5. Kd1, 6. 0-0-0+, 7. Rb1, 8. Rc1, 9. Rd1, 10. Nd1, 11. Nh1, 12. Pa3, 13. Pa4.

What is the position, and what is your estimate of the outcome of the game?

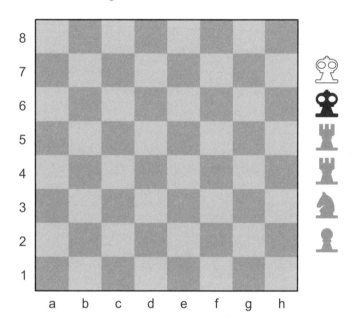

28 ★★☆☆☆

Fill in five missing words so that vertically neighboring letters are identical (they are highlighted by the same colors).

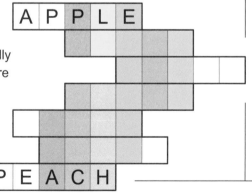

29 ★★★☆☆

Twelve matchsticks form four equilateral triangles. Move two matchsticks to get six equilateral triangles.

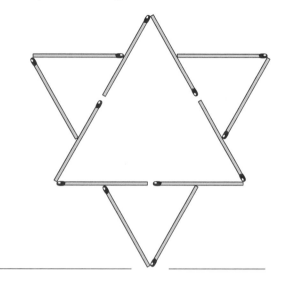

30 ★★★☆☆

Fill in the grid so that each row, column, and stream contains different digits 1 through 6.

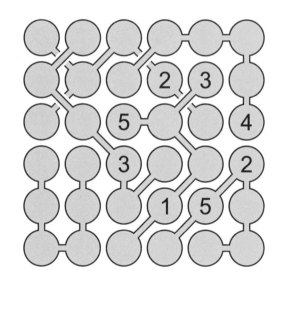

31 ★★★☆☆

Create from the four hexagonal tiles outlines of six regular hexagons. You can rotate pieces, but not overlap.

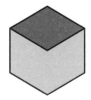

32 ★★★☆☆

Place the digits 1 through 9 (a digit per box) to make both equations true. The larger of two neighboring digits is located higher.

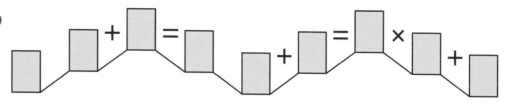

33 ★★☆☆☆

Enter and exit the maze, going under and over.

34 ★★☆☆☆

Divide the shape into five identical parts, cutting along the lines of the grid. Parts may be rotated or reflected.

✂ 5

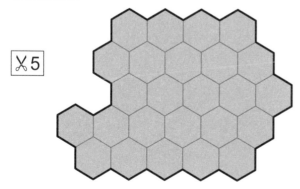

35 ★★★★★

In driving to work one day, Harry noticed that the mileage indicators on his car appeared as shown in the figure below, the left dial showing the mileage (12345.6) since the car was purchased; the right one showing the mileage (123.4) since the dial was last reset to zero. Bear in mind that the left dial can never be reset, and the odometers cannot run backwards when driving in reverse.

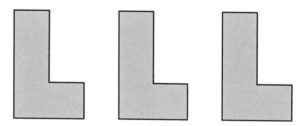

Puzzle 1. If Harry doesn't reset the right-hand dial, what is the least number of miles he must drive before all ten positions show distinct digits (i.e., all ten possible digits are present)?

Puzzle 2. What is the least number of miles until this can happen, if Harry does reset this dial at an appropriate time? The dial may be reset to all 0s, or all 1s, or all 2s, etc.

36 ★★☆☆☆

Can you arrange three L pieces into a symmetrical shape? You can rotate pieces and mirror them, but not overlap.

37 ★★★☆☆

Michael and his three best friends all graduated from high school today! Happy to be out of school, they have a couple of weeks to celebrate and enjoy a whirlwind of graduation parties with friends and family—then it's back to the grindstone. They all have jobs for the summer and then in the fall, they start college. Though they are attending the same college, they've chosen different areas to study, just as they've all lined up different jobs. From the clues, determine each boy's full name, the summer job they've got, and what each has chosen for a major in college.

1. Walt, whose last name isn't Rain, isn't planning to spend the summer landscaping. Michael didn't choose Teaching for a college major.

2. The boy whose last name is Spring plans to major in Finance. Sam isn't a janitor.

3. The boy who chose Business for major is working as a waiter.

4. Paul, whose last name isn't Cloud, didn't sign up for a Business major.

5. The four boys are the boy who's working as a waiter, the boy whose last name is Winter, Paul, and the boy who chose Teaching as a major.

6. Sam chose Engineering for a college major. The boy whose last name is Cloud is working as a technician.

	Cloud	Rain	Spring	Winter	janitor	landscaper	technician	waiter	Business	Engineering	Finance	Teaching
Michael												
Paul												
Sam												
Walt												
Business												
Engineering												
Finance												
Teaching												
janitor												
landscaper												
technician												
waiter												

Use the grid for help.

Use the table for the solution.

First Name	Last Name	Summer Job	College Major

38 ★★★☆☆

Divide the shape into four identical parts, cutting along the lines of the grid. Parts may be rotated or reflected.

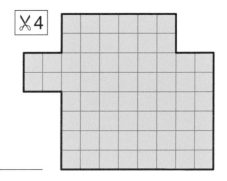

39 ★★☆☆☆

Multiplying my age by 6 then subtracting 6 produces the same result as subtracting 7 from my age then multiplying by 7. How old am I?

40 ★★☆☆☆

Collect all the red targets by rolling the blue ball around the grid. The ball always rolls in a straight line until it hits a wall, and can therefore get trapped. What is the correct sequence of target pickups that allows all targets to be collected?

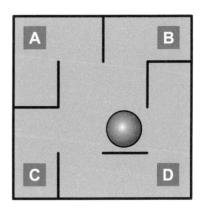

41 ★★★☆☆

Which of the following patterns (A through D) can be folded to create a full, 1 x 1 x 2 block shown in the middle? Parts of the pattern must not overlap each other.

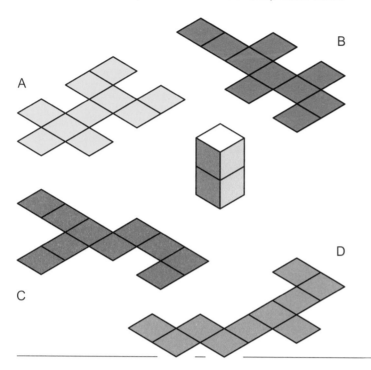

42 ★★★☆☆

Place the ten given letters into the grid so that a chess king could move one square at a time to trace out each of the four given words.

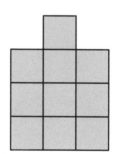

A   E   H
N   O   R
S   T   U
W

NORTH
SOUTH
EAST
WEST

43 ★★☆☆☆

What cheese piece is the odd one out?

44 ★★★★☆

Fill in the grid so that each row, column, and region contains different digits 1 through 8.

	8	5					
	7	6		2	3		
				7	4		
							3
				3	2		5
7				4	1		
5							6
		3	1				4

45 ★★★☆☆

Place the numbers 1 through 10 in the weights so that the whole system balances. Assume the rods and strings are weightless. Heavier weights are never stacked on top of lighter weights.

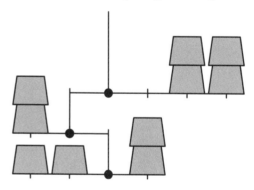

46 ★★★☆☆

Walk the maze from one dot to the other dot.

47 ★★★★☆

Program a robot with a list of movement commands (Up, Down, Left, and Right) to get it from Start to Finish. The robot moves one square at a time in the directions in its program. If the robot bumps into a wall, it performs the next possible move. When it runs out of instructions, it repeats the instructions it has in its cycle. The puzzle has a unique 6-command solution.

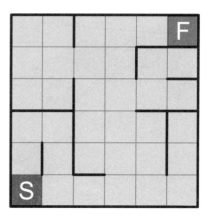

48 ★★★☆☆

Swap two digits to restore the correct equation.

$$4 + 12 \times 7 - 48 = 62$$

49 ★★★★☆

Eight friends A, B, C, D, E, F, G, and H spent a week at a resort center where they had dinner each night, seated at a large circular table. Find seven seating arrangements so that nobody has the same partner on the left at two different meals. Furthermore, nobody has two meals with exactly the same two partners. For example, it cannot be ...BCD.. at one sitting as well as ...DCB.. at another. Sunday's placement is already fixed as shown, and so are half of those for the other six days. Find the remaining placements.

50 ★★★☆☆

Divide the shape into five identical parts, cutting along the lines of the grid. Parts may be rotated or reflected.

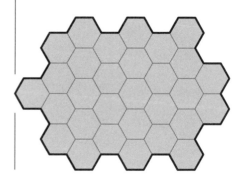

51 ★★★★☆

With three matchsticks divide the house into two parts of the same area. The dividing line must not touch any part of the matchstick A. Whole matchsticks must be used.

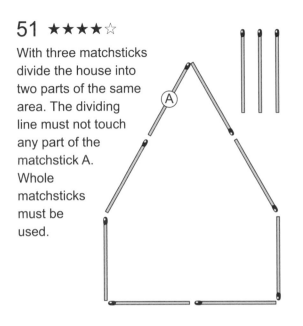

52 ★★☆☆☆

Find the pentagon which has no partner (has no exact twin).

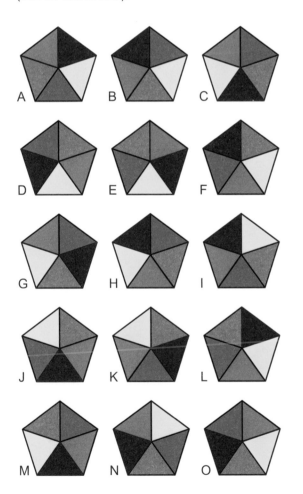

53 ★★★☆☆

In how many ways can four apples be distributed among four people—Addy, Bill, Clint, and Dan?

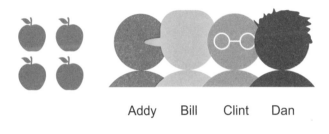

Addy   Bill   Clint   Dan

54 ★★★☆☆

The 3-D shape consists of six solidly colored cubes. Which one of the four 2-D views shown is correct?

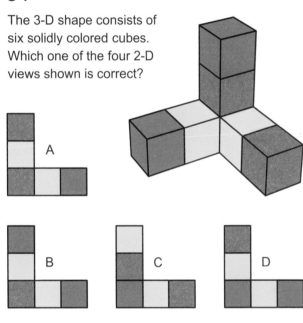

55 ★★☆☆☆

Which piece is not used to build the square shape? Pieces should not be rotated, flipped, or overlap each other.

56 ★★★★☆

In a game, the Black King is on a square that he likes. Unfortunately, he is under attack on that square. Your task is to find a sequence of (normal) moves (but without white moving) for the Black King that will return him to his desired square (a) without subjecting him to check at any time, (b) without taking him to any square (except his present one) more than once, and (c) doing all this in the minimum possible number of moves. On his tour, the Black King can capture some white pieces.

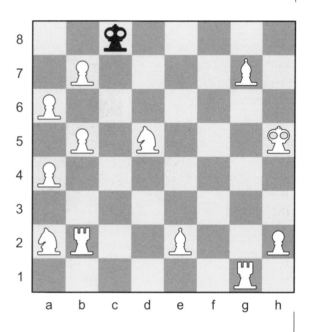

57 ★★★★☆

Divide the shape into four identical parts, cutting along the lines of the grid. Parts may be rotated or reflected.

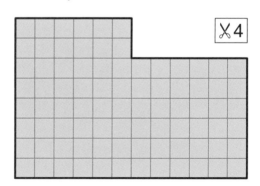

58 ★★★★☆

Following the lines of the grid, connect each pair of identical symbols with a single continuous line. Lines should cover all nodes of the shape, and cannot cross each other.

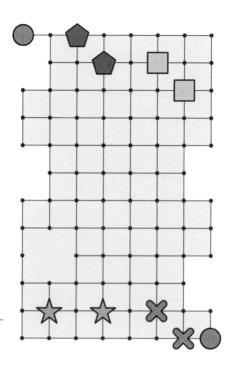

59 ★★☆☆☆

Which composition of two cubes (A through E) should replace the question mark to complete the sequence?

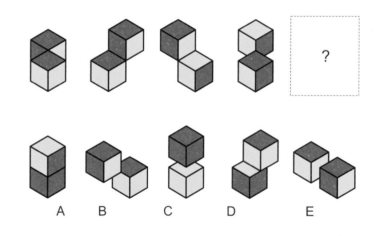

60 ★★★☆☆

Fill in the grid so that each row, column, and region contains different digits 1 through 6.

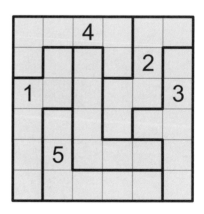

61 ★★☆☆☆

Using all the seven pieces, build up the octagon castle. You can rotate pieces and flip them over, but not overlap.

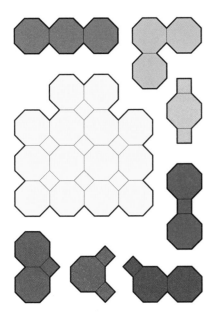

62 ★★★★★

If the integers from 1 to 5000 are listed in equivalence classes according to the number of written characters (including blanks and hyphens) needed to write them out in full in correct English, there are exactly forty such nonempty classes.

For example, class "4" contains three numbers (4, 5, and 9), since FOUR, FIVE, and NINE are the only such numbers that can be written out with exactly four characters. Similarly, class "42" contains nine numbers (3373, 3377, 3378, 3773, 3777, 3778, 3873, 3877, and 3878). Find the unique class "n" that contains just one number.

63 ★★★★☆

Summer has finally arrived! To celebrate the occasion, Dan and Janet Smith decided to throw a barbeque and afternoon party at their summerhouse on Fiesta Lake. Telling all their friends to bring their family, friends, and of course bathing suits, they ended up with quite a houseful and the party was a great success. The Smiths were especially pleased because some of their relatives who lived farther away managed to attend. Determine from the clues the full name of the family members in attendance, their relationship to Dan and Janet Smith, and the city where each had their home.

1. Natalie, whose last name wasn't West, didn't live in Boston.
2. Janet's cousin didn't live in New York, though her last name was Mann.
3. George didn't live in Providence. Sara's last name wasn't Green.
4. Robert, who was Dan's uncle, didn't live in New York. Ms. Green lived in New York.
5. Sara wasn't Janet's sister. Mr. Smith wasn't related to Janet.
6. Dan's brother lived in Chicago. The man whose last name is West lives in Providence.

	Green	Mann	Smith	West	Dan's brother	Dan's uncle	Janet's cousin	Janet's sister	Boston	Chicago	New York	Providence
George												
Natalie												
Robert												
Sara												
Boston												
Chicago												
New York												
Providence												
Dan's brother												
Dan's uncle												
Janet's cousin												
Janet's sister												

Use the grid for help.

Use the table for the solution.

First Name	Last Name	Relationship	Home City

64 ★★☆☆☆

Solve the maze turning left or right (only) at red nodes (only). U-turns are not permitted.

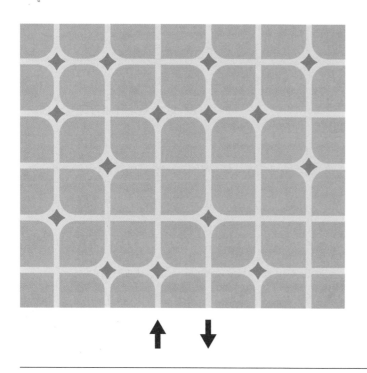

65 ★★★☆☆

Which die can be formed by folding the given pattern along the dotted lines?

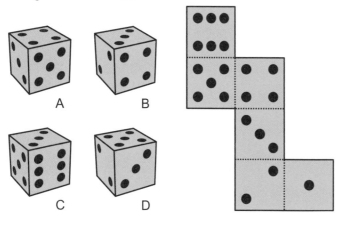

A B C D

66 ★★★☆☆

Swap two digits to restore the correct equation.

$$7 \times 7 + 9 \times 9 = 1\ 3\ 8$$

67 ★★☆☆☆

Bubbles of which color cover the least total area?

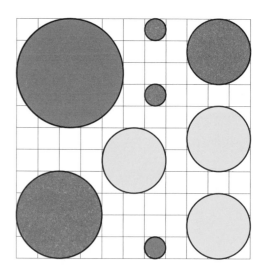

68 ★★★☆☆

How many times does the wire shape appear in the grid in any possible orientation, including rotations and reflections?

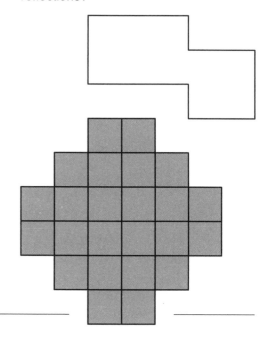

22

69 ★★☆☆☆

Using the six bricks, build a wall with two "domino windows", one horizontal (2 x 1) and one vertical (1 x 2). The windows must be separate, completely surrounded by bricks, and may not touch each other or the perimeter of the structure, even at a corner. You *cannot* rotate bricks, flip, and/or overlap them.

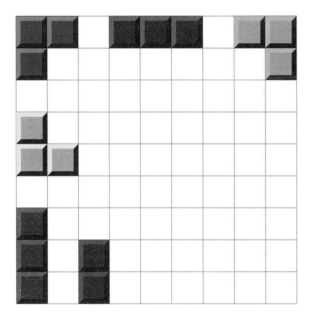

Use the grid to draw the answer.

70 ★★★★☆

Slide each weight half a unit distance left or right, and then put the digits 1 through 7 into the weights so that the whole system balances. Assume the rods and strings are weightless.

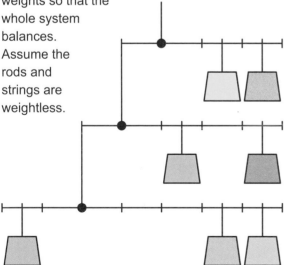

71 ★★★★☆

Fill in the grid so that each row, column, and stream contains different digits 1 through 7.

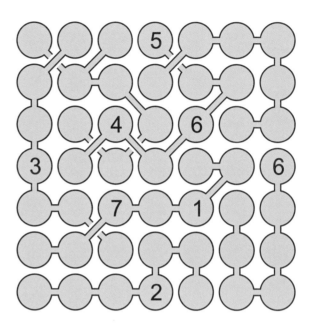

72 ★★☆☆☆

In each of the sentences below is the name of an animal; it occurs in a string of consecutive letters. Can you find the animal?

The dandelions are plentiful in the front yard this year!

- - - - - - - - - - - - - - - - - - - -

"We want eaters!" exclaimed the organizer of the County Fair Pie Contest.

- - - - - - - - - - - - - - - - - - - -

In Japan, there are many different holidays.

- - - - - - - - - - - - - - - - - - - -

"Please Jack, allow me," said the chauffeur, opening the door for his employer.

- - - - - - - - - - - - - - - - - - - -

Amy got terrific grades on her report card this semester!

- - - - - - - - - - - - - - - - - - - -

"See that mark you made? Erase it, right now!" ordered the teacher.

73 ★★☆☆☆

Fill in the blanks.   _u_ _ _ _ro_ _ _o_ _u_ _ _ over _he _ _ _ _ _o_.

74 ★★★☆☆

Tonight the teashop in town, Bags with Riches, is having a tea-fest. Along with tasty snacks and pastries, they'll have a number of different teas available for customers to try, free of charge. Determine the full name of each person working at the teashop, the favorite flavored tea of each worker, and the snack each worker made for the event.

1. Ms. Croupe didn't like the Russian caravan tea. Travis brought cinnamon rolls.

2. The worker who brought apple crisp didn't like peppermint tea.

3. Lindsay, whose last name wasn't Tanner, didn't bring the chocolate chip cookies. Martin didn't like orange pekoe tea.

4. Lindsay's last name is Manor.

5. The four workers are Sheila, the one who likes green tea, Mr. Walker, and the man who brought peanut butter fudge.

6. The person who loved peppermint tea brought chocolate chip cookies.

	Croupe	Manor	Tanner	Walker	green tea	orange pekoe tea	peppermint tea	Russian caravan tea	apple crisp	chocolate chip cookies	cinnamon rolls	peanut butter fudge
Lindsay												
Martin												
Sheila												
Travis												
apple crisp												
chocolate chip cookies												
cinnamon rolls												
peanut butter fudge												
green tea												
orange pekoe tea												
peppermint tea												
Russian caravan tea												

Use the grid for help.

Use the table for the solution.

First Name	Last Name	Flavored Teas	Snacks

75 ★★☆☆☆

What is the maximum number of green chairs, that can be placed in the pink room? Chairs can be rotated and/or flipped over, but not overlapped.

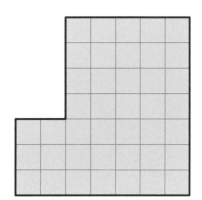

76 ★★☆☆☆

Club member numbers are on transparent badges. Two badges are overlaid, making what looks like 89. Neither badge has 8 or 9, but the sum of the badges is 89. What are the numbers?

77 ★★★☆☆

Put three 1s, three 2s, three 3s, and three 4s in the circles. If a circle contains the number **n**, then the *shortest* distance to another circle containing the same number must be **n**. The distance between two circles is the smallest number of lines you need to traverse to get from one to the other.

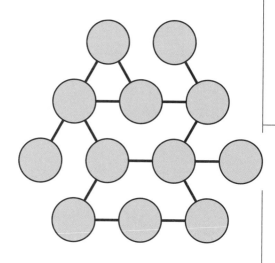

78 ★★★★★

Divide the shape into four identical parts, cutting along the lines of the grid. Parts may be rotated or reflected.

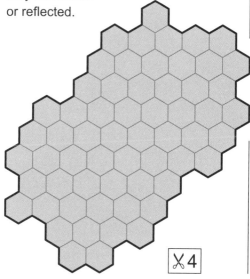

✂4

79 ★★☆☆☆

Place eight cards in a line to form a real 9-letter word. Cards can overlap each other but no card should be fully covered, rotated, or flipped over.

Example: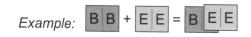

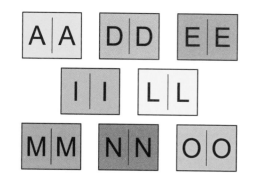

Use the row for the solution.

80 ★★☆☆☆

What should the thirtieth disc be?

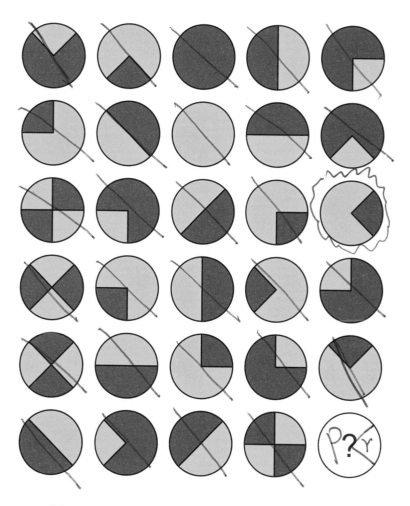

25

81 ★★★☆☆

Color a subset of the arrows below such that each white arrow points at exactly one other white arrow and each colored arrow points at exactly two other colored arrows.

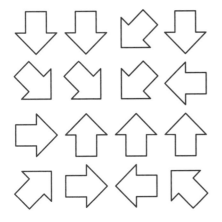

82 ★★☆☆☆

Place letters in the empty squares to get twelve words reading across and down.

M	O	S	T
G	E	N	E
T	U	N	A
R	E	E	S

83 ★★★★☆

Fill in the grid so that each row, column, and region contains different digits 1 through 8.

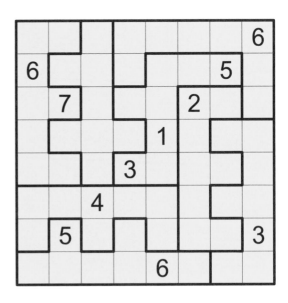

84 ★★★☆☆

Arrange the numbers 0 through 9 in the circles so that no two consecutive numbers are connected by a straight line.

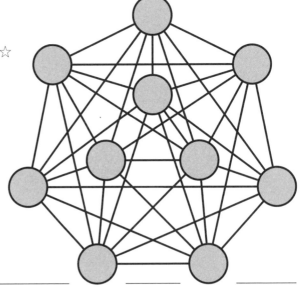

85 ★★☆☆☆

Following the lines of the grid, connect each pair of identical symbols with a single continuous line. Lines should cover all nodes of the shape, and cannot cross each other.

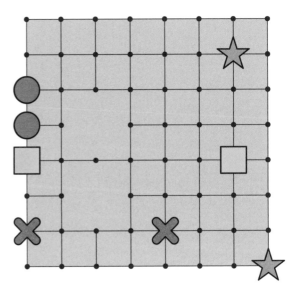

86 ★★★★☆

How many isosceles triangles (including equilateral ones) of any size and orientation can you find in the shape? To count, the triangle must have three coins placed exactly at its respective vertices.

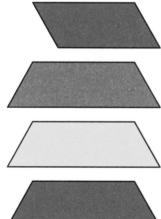

87 ★★☆☆☆

Arrange these six pieces into a plain equilateral triangle so that pieces of the same color do not touch each other even at a corner. You can rotate pieces, but not overlap.

88 ★★☆☆☆

Four squares (two blue, one yellow, and one red) are overlapped. If the area of the yellow square is 1, what's the total area of the dark brown intersection parts?

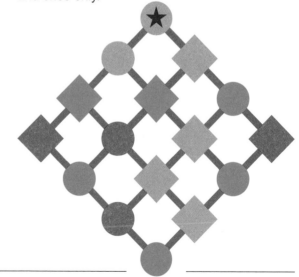

89 ★★☆☆☆

Starting from the top-green atom, jump to any unvisited atom that matches either in shape or color (or both). Each move must be along the grid's line but may leap over other atoms in that line. Find a route that visits every atom once and once only.

90 ★★★☆☆

What is the next number in the series?

4   8   9   14   15   12   24   21   22   ?

91 ★★☆☆☆

The shape consists of four blocks. Which is bigger - the total volume of the yellow blocks or the total volume of the green blocks?

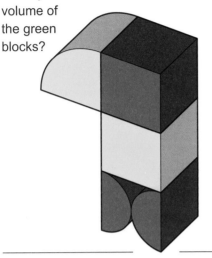

92 ★★★☆☆

Draw a path from start (S) to finish (F). The width of the path is one square. The path moves horizontally and vertically, and does not touch itself, even diagonally. Each chess piece attacks the same number of segments of the path.

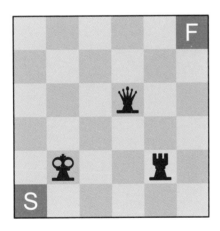

93 ★★★☆☆

Saturday, the local church held a big auction to raise money for local charities. The day was a big success with lots of treasures and lots of bidding. Sally and three others were especially pleased with their purchases. Determine the full name of each person, the item each won, and how much each paid for it.

1. Sally, whose last name wasn't Vialle, didn't bid on the gold necklace but she won a more expensive item than the antique clock.

2. Mr. Parson won the most expensive item, which was $100.

3. Abigail's item was more expensive than the one Tom won but less expensive than the music box.

4. The Victorian lamp was won for $75, but Mark didn't win it.

5. Tom, whose last name isn't Welsh, won the $25 item. The $50 item was won by Ms. Smart.

6. Abigail didn't win the antique clock.

Use the grid for help.

	Parson	Smart	Vialle	Welsh	antique clock	gold necklace	music box	Victorian lamp	$25	$50	$75	$100
Abigail												
Mark												
Sally												
Tom												
$25												
$50												
$75												
$100												
antique clock												
gold necklace												
music box												
Victorian lamp												

Use the table for the solution.

First Name	Last Name	Item Won	Amount Paid

94 ★★☆☆☆

What do these words have in common?

BALL LEST MISS POT TUN

95 ★★★★☆

Divide the shape into four identical parts, cutting along the lines of the grid. Parts may be rotated or reflected.

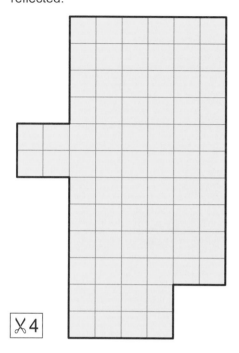

✂4

96 ★★★☆☆

Which four pieces should be used to form the bowl shown in the middle? You can rotate pieces and flip them over, but not overlap.

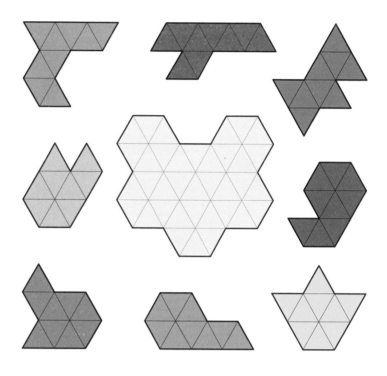

97 ★★★★★

Put into each empty box a positive integer so that the resulting thirteen arithmetic statements, vertical, horizontal, and diagonal (NW to SE), are true.

$$\boxed{} + \boxed{5} + \boxed{} = \boxed{}$$
$$+ \quad \times \quad + \quad \times \quad + \quad = \quad +$$
$$\boxed{} + \boxed{} + \boxed{} = \boxed{}$$
$$+ \quad \times \quad + \quad \times \quad + \quad = \quad +$$
$$\boxed{} + \boxed{} + \boxed{} = \boxed{}$$
$$= \quad = \quad = \quad = \quad = \quad = \quad =$$
$$\boxed{} + \boxed{} + \boxed{} = \boxed{57}$$

98 ★★☆☆☆

Fill in the grid so that each row, column, and stream contains different digits 1 through 5.

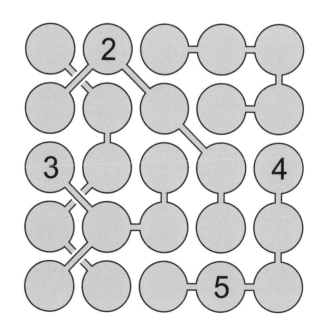

29

99 ★★★☆☆

Travel the metro from your home station (E) to the office (G). Beware, all trains stop every third station only. For example, from E you can only exit or change at stations C and P.

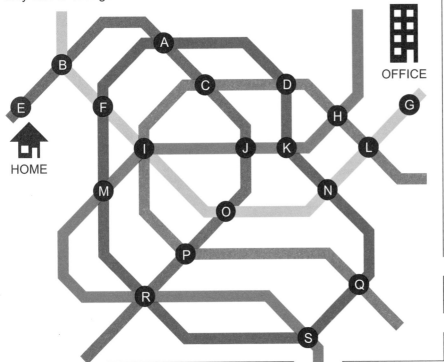

100 ★★☆☆☆

Place eight cards in a line to form a real 9-letter word. Cards can overlap each other but no card should be fully covered, rotated, or flipped over.

Example: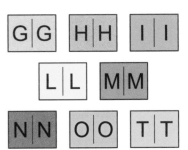

101 ★★☆☆☆

Fill in the grid so that each row, column, and region contains different digits 1 through 5.

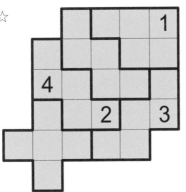

102 ★★★☆☆

On my broken calculator with keys + − ÷ x =, the only functional number is 7. How can I get 34 to appear in the readout?

103 ★★★☆☆

Arrange the pieces of LEL to make some shape, and then make the same shape using the pieces of ELE. You can rotate pieces and flip them over, but not overlap.

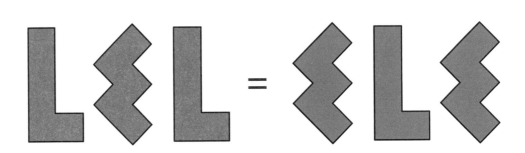

104 ★★☆☆☆

Swap two digits to restore the correct equation.

$$12 + 12 \times 13 = 157$$

105 ★★★☆☆

Following the lines of the grid, connect each pair of identical symbols with a single continuous line. Lines should cover all nodes of the shape, and cannot cross each other.

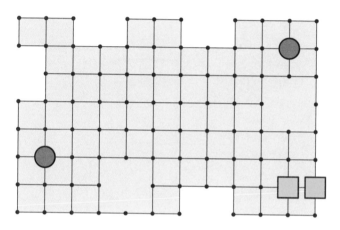

106 ★★★★★

The circles are located at the corners of a collection of equilateral triangles. No two triangles share a corner, though they may share part of an edge. Determine which vertices go together to form the triangles.

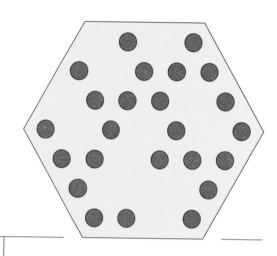

107 ★★★★☆

Using all the twenty triangles of the five pentagons, make a single large plain pentagon to match the one shown. No triangles of the same color are allowed to touch each other even at a corner. Note that the grid within the large pentagon is provided just for your convenience. Not all of the grid's lines are to be used.

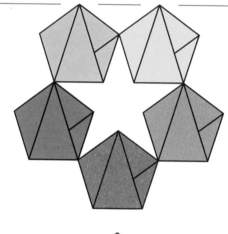

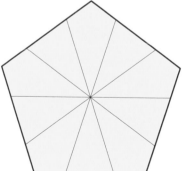

108 ★★★★★

Divide the shape into five identical parts, cutting along the lines of the grid. Parts may be rotated or reflected.

✂ 5

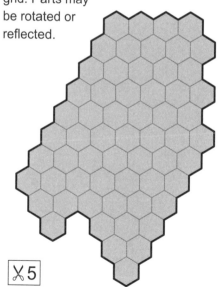

109 ★★★☆☆

Fill in the grid so that each row, column, and stream contains different digits 1 through 7.

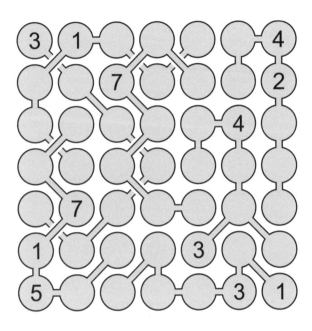

110 ★★★★☆

In the domino rectangle, trace a connected island of seven adjacent dominoes which contain two blank squares, two 1s, ..., two 5s, and two 6s.

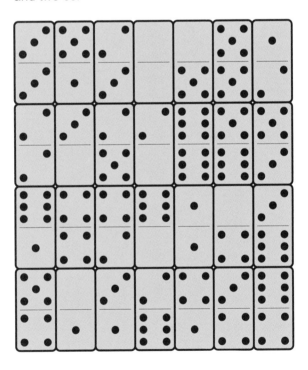

111 ★★★☆☆

Add the letters of PRIMATE to the puzzle on the right so that a chess king could move one square at a time to spell out the phrase "One man's meat is another man's poison."

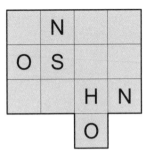

112 ★★★★☆

Divide the shape into four identical parts, cutting along the lines of the grid. Parts may be rotated or reflected.

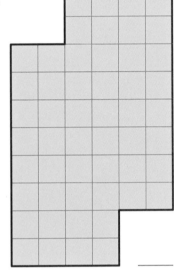

113 ★★☆☆☆

Which pattern, when folded along the dotted lines, forms the block shown in the center? No parts of the pattern should overlap each other.

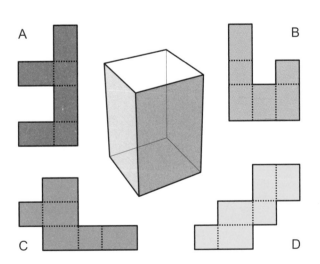

114 ★★★☆☆

Summer's here and it's hot outside! Yesterday, Sara invited three of her friends over for a day of fun in the sun, and of course, in the pool. She had the day all planned with lots of food, activities, and frolic time in the pool between events. A good time was had by all and at the end of the day, her friends agreed the party was a great success. Determine each girl's full name, the activity each won, and the color of each girl's bathing suit.

1. Ms. Wilson, whose first name wasn't Sheila, didn't wear a black bathing suit. Sherry Sanford didn't win the underwater swim.

2. The girl in the purple bathing suit won the croquet game.

3. Sherry didn't wear a green bathing suit.

4. Ms. Norton, whose first name wasn't Sara, didn't win the water balloon toss. Samantha didn't win the game of croquet.

5. Sara's bathing suit was blue but her last name wasn't Wilson. Sheila didn't win any of the water games.

6. The girl with the black bathing suit won the water relay. Ms. Grimes didn't win the underwater swim.

Use the grid for help.

	Grimes	Norton	Sanford	Wilson	croquet	underwater swim	water balloon toss	water relay	black	blue	green	purple
Samantha												
Sara												
Sheila												
Sherry												
black												
blue												
green												
purple												
croquet												
underwater swim												
water balloon toss												
water relay												

Use the table for the solution.

First Name	Last Name	Activity	Color

115 ★★☆☆☆

A country mints four denominations of coins, in whole numbers of cents. It takes four of these coins to make 21¢, or 24¢, or 25¢, or 26¢. What are the denominations of coins?

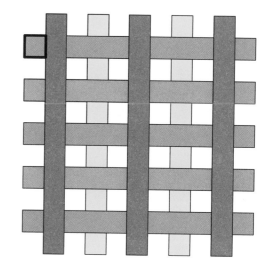

117 ★★☆☆☆

How many outlines of squares of all sizes can you count in the grid? One square is already shown.

116 ★★☆☆☆

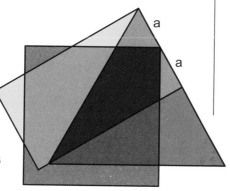

The yellow rectangle, blue square, and red triangle are overlapped. If the area of the red triangle is 1, what's the area of the brown intersection part? The two edge sections **a** are equal in length.

118 ★★☆☆☆

Eight matchsticks form two arrows pointing in different directions. Move three matchsticks to make the arrows point in the same direction.

119 ★★★☆☆

Fill in the grid so that each row, column, and region contains different digits 1 through 7.

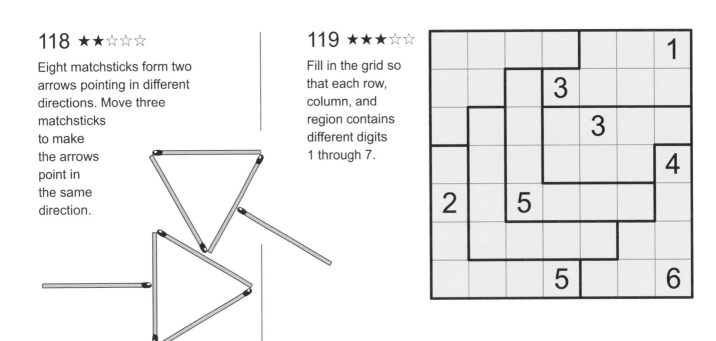

120 ★★☆☆☆

In this maze you can step only to a face that is looking directly at you. Start on the top happy face and step any distance in a row or column to a sad face. Then alternate happy, sad, happy, sad... etc. The aim is to reach the top sad face. For example, the only valid first step is to the sad face with the red nose. There are then three possible moves (happy faces with red-noses) for the second move. After that you are on your own!

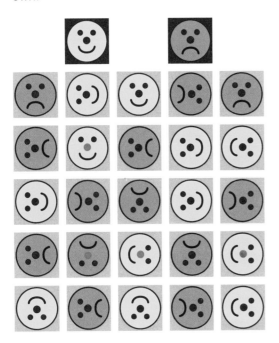

121 ★★★★☆

Rotate and rearrange these strips so that four valid equations appear across the four rows. In each equation, operations are done from left to right.

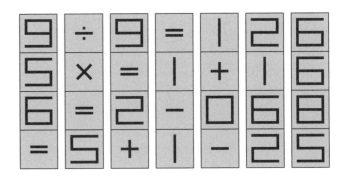

122 ★★★★☆

You have a number comprising all the ten digits, ABCDEFGHIJ. It is divided into eight triplets: ABC, BCD, CDE, DEF, EFG, FGH, GHI, and HIJ. The first of them should be divisible by 2, the second by 3, and so on, so that the last triplet is divisible by 9. Example: Consider 3207654189. Here 320/2, 207/3, 076/4, 765/5, 654/6, and 189/9 are all integers, but 541/7 and 418/8 are not. Find all permutations of the ten decimal digits, for which each of the eight triplets is divisible by its designated divisor.

123 ★★★★☆

Place numbers 1 through 15 in the green circles so that the distance from 1 to 2, 2 to 3, 3 to 4 and so on increases each time.

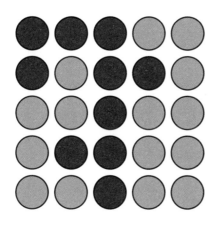

124 ★★☆☆☆

Divide the diamond into six parts of the same area, cutting along the lines of the grid.

Puzzle 1. All the six parts are identical. They may be rotated or reflected.

Puzzle 2. All the six parts are different.

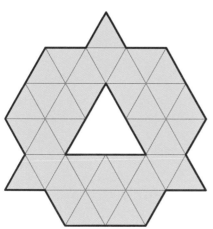

125 ★★★☆☆

Which of the four shapes cannot be formed by using all five of the pieces on the right? Pieces can be rotated, but not flipped over or overlapped.

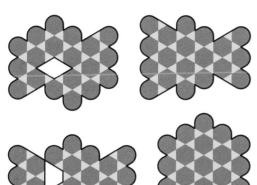

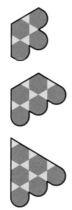

126 ★★★★★

The puzzle is quite like a crossword puzzle, with clues across and down. The difference is that the clues are about numbers, and the blank squares are filled with digits.

In the problem below, each of the letters R through Y stands for a positive integer (which may have many digits). All the numbers A through E are to be represented in decimal, and no numbers are allowed to have leading zeroes; this implies that a zero digit may not fill a space with a letter in it. Each blank square is to contain a single digit. Thus, for example, "A across" will be a 7-digit integer.

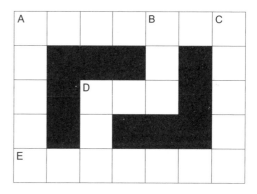

Across:
$A = R! + S$
$D = X - Y - R$
$E = W^W / T$

Down:
$A = T^S$
$B = X + X + X + X$
$C = X * X - Y$
$D = Y$

127 ★★☆☆☆

A series of letters, following its own logical rules, starts with:

AS BR CQ

In the course of the series, there are two instances of double letters. What are they?

128 ★★★☆☆

Four friends went on their annual fishing trip this past weekend. The trip heralded the end of summer and is usually their last chance to spend a weekend together before family, school, and work draws them away to other concerns. This year was an unusually good year for the fishing part of the trip and they all arrived home with a few new fish stories to add to their growing collection. Determine the full name of each friend, the size of each friend's biggest catch (48 pounds to 52 pounds), and what type of fish each caught.

1. Sam's last name wasn't Harmon.

2. Charlie, whose last name wasn't Remane, didn't catch the smallest fish.

3. The man who caught the 50-pound fish didn't catch the bluegill.

4. Mr. Warner didn't catch the 49-pound trout.

5. The flounder was caught by Norm.

6. The fish were caught in the following order, from smallest to largest: Mr. Harmon, George Blue, bass, and Charlie.

	Blue	Harmon	Remane	Warner	48 pounds	49 pounds	50 pounds	52 pounds	bass	bluegill	flounder	trout
Charlie												
George												
Norm												
Sam												
bass												
bluegill												
flounder												
trout												
48 pounds												
49 pounds												
50 pounds												
52 pounds												

Use the grid for help.

Use the table for the solution.

First Name	Last Name	Fish Size	Fish Type

129 ★★☆☆☆

Swap two digits to restore the correct equation.

$$4 + 6 - 2 \times 5 + 9 = 12$$

130 ★★☆☆☆

Fill in six missing words so that vertically neighboring letters are identical (they are highlighted by the same colors).

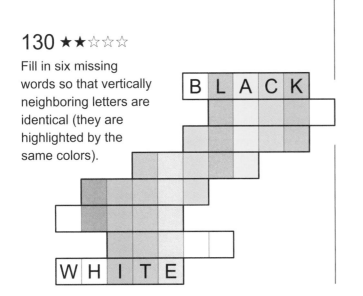

B L A C K

W H I T E

131 ★★★★☆

Divide the shape into four identical parts, cutting along the lines of the grid. Parts may be rotated or reflected.

✄4

132 ★★★★☆

The shape consisting of thirteen equal balls is inscribed into a sphere. The inner ball is surrounded by twelve balls and it touches each of them. This shape is one of the two tightest packings of thirteen balls in a sphere of the minimal radius. The shape can be split into three flat layers in two distinct ways, as shown. Now, there are several puzzles.

Puzzle A. How many straight lines of three balls can you count in the shape?

Puzzle B. How many equilateral triangles of any size and orientation can you spot in the shape? To count, an equilateral triangle must have three balls whose centers lie exactly at its three corners.

Puzzle C. How many squares of any size and orientation can you spot in the shape? To count, a square must have four balls whose centers lie exactly at its four corners.

Puzzle D. What is the ratio between the total volume of all the thirteen balls and the sphere?

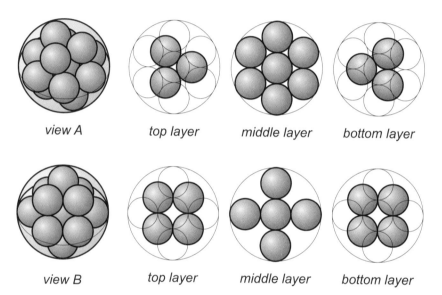

| view A | top layer | middle layer | bottom layer |

| view B | top layer | middle layer | bottom layer |

133 ★★☆☆☆

Nine window frames are scattered into a pile. Determine the sequence in which they should be removed from the topmost one all the way down to the one at the bottom of the pile.

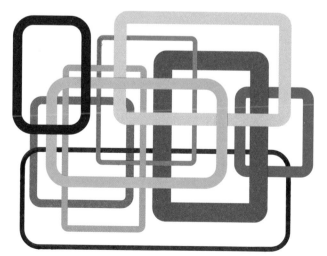

134 ★★★★☆

A shape can be divided into seven unequally sized pieces with three lines, following the grid lines. No line crosses itself, and each crosses the other lines just once. Following these rules, divide the shape into seven equally sized pieces with three lines.

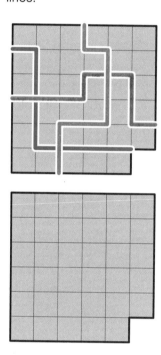

135 ★★☆☆☆

Put into each empty box a digit so that all the six indicated equations, vertical and horizontal, are true. One digit is already shown.

$$\square + \square = \square$$
$$-\quad \times \quad \div$$
$$\square + \square = \square$$
$$=\quad =\quad =$$
$$\square \div 3 = \square$$

136 ★★☆☆☆

Using the given letters, restore the famous idiom. The same letters are marked by identical colors/digits on the bottom.

  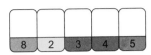

137 ★★☆☆☆

Enter the maze from the yellow stepping stone on the left. Take three steps on blue and then change color. Take three steps on the new color and change again. Repeat this sequence, changing color every third step, until you can reach the red exit stone on the right.

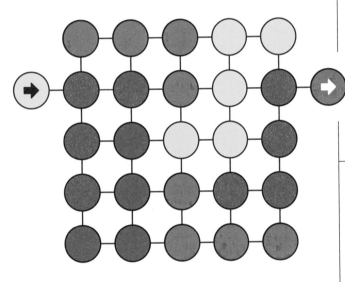

139 ★★★★☆

Divide the shape into four identical parts, cutting along the lines of the grid. Parts may be rotated or reflected.

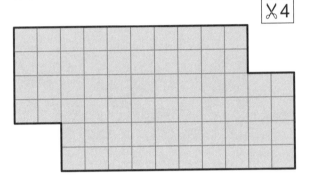

140 ★★☆☆☆

Three of the four line networks are identical. Which one differs?

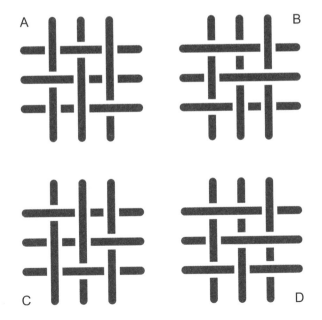

138 ★★★☆☆

Which pattern forms a full cube when folded along the dotted lines? No parts of the patterns should overlap each other.

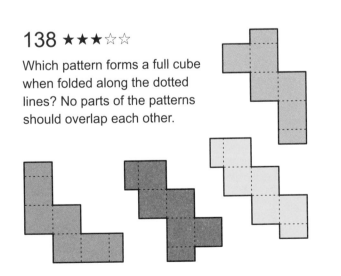

141 ★★★☆☆

By multiplying the digits of 679, it takes five steps to get to a single figure, as shown. What are the smallest numbers for which it takes three and four steps?

679

step 1:
$$6 \times 7 \times 9 = 378$$

step 2:
$$3 \times 7 \times 8 = 168$$

step 3:
$$1 \times 6 \times 8 = 48$$

step 4:
$$4 \times 8 = 32$$

step 5:
$$3 \times 2 = 6$$

142 ★★★★☆

Exchange the position of the black and blue pieces in the fewest number of moves/jumps. A piece moves into the nearest free spot or jumps through the neighboring piece into the free spot immediately behind that neighboring one. Black and blue pieces move in turns.

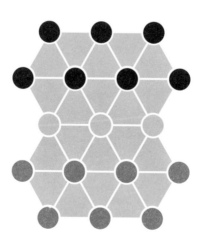

143 ★★★☆☆

Fill in the grid so that each row, column, and stream contains different digits 1 through 6.

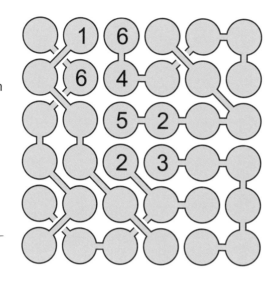

144 ★★★★★

It is (perhaps not well) known that there are no more than 100 prime numbers whose digits are strictly increasing in magnitude. There should be at least two digits in such a number. Examples are 59, 457, 2789, 23459, 345689, and 1235789. Among these, some are reversible; that is, they are also primes when written backwards. Only the two largest such primes have more than five digits; both of them are shown above—345689, and 1235789. Solve some challenges with such primes.

   Easy challenge. Find all the strictly increasing reversible primes within numbers 1 through 100.

   Moderate challenge. Find all the strictly increasing reversible primes within numbers 1 through 1000.

   Hard challenge. Find all the strictly increasing reversible primes which have four digits.

   Hardest challenge. Find all the strictly increasing reversible primes which have five digits.

   A hint. While searching for primes, it is useful to remember that none of the primes (except 2 and 5) has 0, 2, 4, 5, 6, or 8 as its rightmost digit.

145 ★★★☆☆

Place the seven chess pieces on a chess board so that no piece attacks any other.

146 ★★☆☆☆

Rotate the four joined circles around the center so that all the letters form a famous 5-word proverb. Each word should read from the biggest circle to the center.

Use the table for the solution.

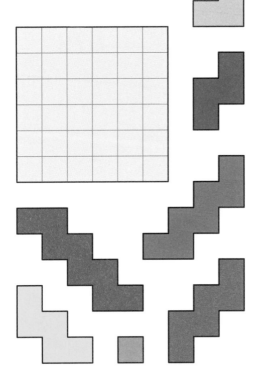

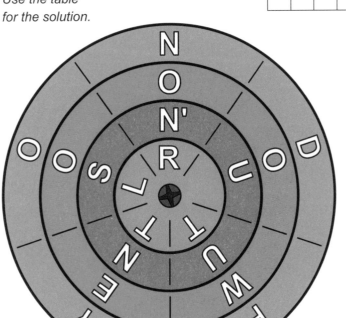

147 ★★☆☆☆

Fit all pieces within the shape. You can rotate pieces and flip them over, but not overlap.

148 ★★★☆☆

The shape consists of six blocks. Which is greater— the total volume of the light blocks or the total volume of the dark blocks?

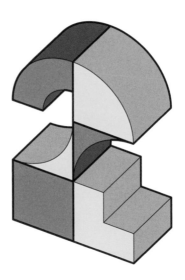

149 ★★☆☆☆

Place eight cards in a line to form a real 9-letter word. Cards can overlap each other but no card should be fully covered, rotated, or flipped.

Example:

150 ★★★★☆

Divide the Cap with two matchsticks into two parts of the same area.

151 ★★★☆☆

A superstitious pool player didn't like 8-ball, so he had a 16-ball set specially made. When he racked the balls up, he always arranged them so the each ball was the difference of the 2 balls above it. Can you find the arrangement he used?

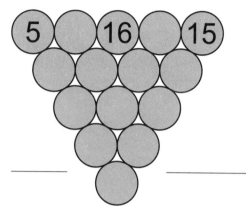

152 ★★★☆☆

Going through adjacent squares, find a path from Start to Finish that passes through an equal number of squares of each (non-white) color. You may visit the white square. Visit no square more than once.

153 ★★★☆☆

Four residents of Park Street all left for vacation on Sunday evening. Each family left behind a pet, whom one of the local teenagers had agreed to take care of for them. Kristin, the local teenager, made a schedule of stops for each day to cover the four different pets she needed to take care of that week. Determine the last name of each family, the name of each pet, what type of animal it was, and in what order each pet was visited each day.

1. The Fords didn't leave Nobs. The parrot was visited last.
2. The first pet fed wasn't the horse, but the horse was fed just before Cutie.
3. The O'Henry family was the first stop, but a cat wasn't fed there. Puck wasn't the Smith family pet.
4. The dog wasn't called Nobs. The cat's name was Puck.
5. The last pet visited wasn't Nobs.
6. The Walkers didn't own a horse, but their pet was the second one fed. Cutie is the name of the parrot.

	Cutie	Nobs	Puck	Toby	cat	dog	horse	parrot	1st	2nd	3rd	4th
Ford												
O'Henry												
Smith												
Walker												
1st												
2nd												
3rd												
4th												
cat												
dog												
horse												
parrot												

Use the grid for help.

Use the table for the solution.

Last Name	Pet Name	Pet Type	Order Visited

154 ★★★☆☆

For each of these two elements find another two elements so that the elements in each triplet have no common letters with their counterparts.

GOLD		

ZINC		

155 ★★☆☆☆

Nine digits 1 through 9 are partly visible. Restore the digits, knowing that the cells with even digits form a tetromino, and cells with odd digits from a pentomino.

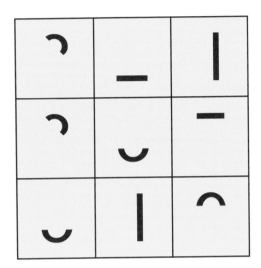

156 ★★★☆☆

Using a right-angled triangle ruler without marks and a pencil, can you draw an equilateral triangle?

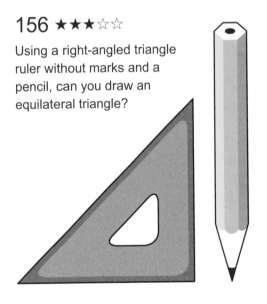

157 ★★☆☆☆

Get from top-left A to bottom-right C, stepping one tile at a time (up, down, left, or right) and repeating the sequence AABBC-...-AABBC.

158 ★★★★☆

Divide the shape into five identical parts, cutting along the lines of the grid. Parts may be rotated or reflected.

✂5

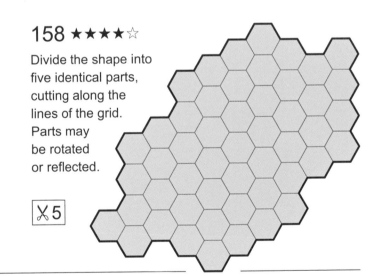

159 ★★★☆☆

Put a digit in each box so that the equation is true. The boxes should also balance, where each digit represents the weight of that box. Assume the weight of the bar is negligible.

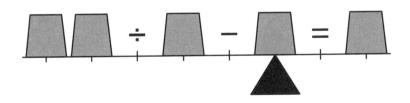

42

160 ★★★★☆

A tour joins up dots in a loop with straight lines. An example of a longest tour (a loop of the longest total length) is shown on the left. For each set of twelve points in the middle and on the right, find the longest tour.

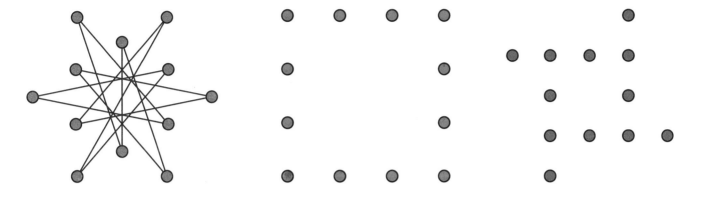

161 ★★★☆☆

Place the thirteen given letters into the grid so that a chess king could move one square at a time to trace out each of the four given words.

SUMMER
AUTUMN
WINTER
SPRING

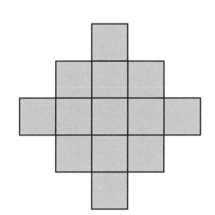

A E G I M
M N P R S
T U W

163 ★★☆☆☆

In what way can you interpret this statement to make it true?

1240 = 2021

164 ★★★☆☆

Fill in the grid so that each row, column, and stream contains different digits 1 through 6.

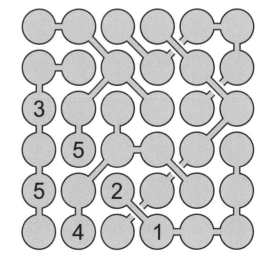

162 ★★★☆☆

Five identical cubes are arranged as shown. What two letters should replace the two question marks?

43

165 ★★★★☆

Substitute digits for the letters so as to make a "correct" division statement in decimal arithmetic. The same numerical digit must be substituted for each occurrence of a given letter, and no digit may be used for two different letters. The leading (leftmost) digit of each number formed cannot be zero. Each box is just a place holder and may have any but must have some digit placed within. Hint: L = 8.

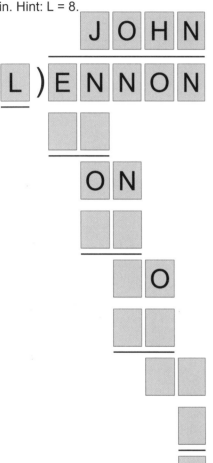

166 ★★☆☆☆

 Example:

Place seven cards in a line to form a real 8-letter word. Cards can overlap each other but no card should be fully covered, rotated, or flipped.

A A B B E E L L

M M R R U U

167 ★★☆☆☆

Three of the four triangle networks are identical. Which one differs?

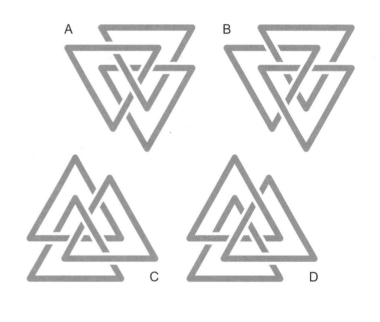

168 ★★★☆☆

Arrange the six L-shaped pieces in a 4 x 6 board so that all the twelve dots are connected. You may rotate and mirror the pieces.

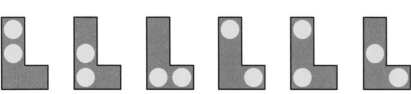

169 ★★★★☆

What is the longest sentence-like sequence of words with all of its letters placed in alphabetical order? Same letter can be used several times. For example:

BE MY

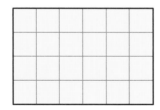

170 ★★★☆☆

Even though she forgot her shopping list, Harriet spent the morning grocery shopping for her family. Being the forgetful sort, forgetting her list was not that unusual, just a bit inconvenient. She didn't usually have too much trouble with the grocery shopping because her four kids accompanied her and were used to reminding her when she forgot something. For their help, she always let each of the children add one favorite food to the cart. This week as a special treat, she took them all out for ice cream on the way home. Determine the name of each child and the favorite food each selected, what each child helped their mom remember, and what flavor of ice cream each child got in their ice cream cone.

1. The child that got mocha almond ice cream also had peanut butter cookies. Peter remembered the paper towels.

2. The girl who remembered the roast beef got coffee ice cream. Cindy got blueberries for her favorite food.

3. Barry didn't get the chocolate bar. Rose didn't like coffee ice cream.

4. Peter didn't have peanut butter cookies but he did get strawberry ice cream.

5. Cindy didn't remember that her mom needed to buy bread. Barry didn't get the vanilla ice cream.

6. Barry didn't remember the carrots. Rose didn't like graham crackers or mocha almond ice cream.

	Blueberries	Chocolate bar	Graham crackers	Peanut butter cookies	bread	carrots	paper towels	roast beef	coffee	mocha almond	strawberry	vanilla
Barry												
Cindy												
Peter												
Rose												
coffee												
mocha almond												
strawberry												
vanilla												
bread												
carrots												
paper towels												
roast beef												

Use the grid for help.

Use the table for the solution.

Child's Name	Favorite Food	Forgotten Item	Ice Cream

171 ★★★☆☆

Divide the shape into four identical parts, cutting along the lines of the grid. Parts may be rotated or reflected.

✂ 4

172 ★★★★☆

Put three of the cards in the top row to make a true equation. Then rearrange those cards with one additional card to make a different true equation in the next row. Continue adding a card until you have made a true equation from all the cards. No card should be used twice in a given row.

$3-2$	$8 \div 4$	$9+4$

3×3	$7-8$

$4=5$

45

173 ★★★★☆

Travel from left (A) to right (B) on the yellow paths, and then back (to A) via purple. Note the twelve bridges where paths cross.

A

B

174 ★★☆☆☆

Which is the odd one out?

175 ★★★☆☆

Two equilateral triangles are inscribed in a big equilateral triangle, each one with a 30-degree, clockwise turn. What is the ratio between the total area of all the dark parts of the middle triangle and the total light area?

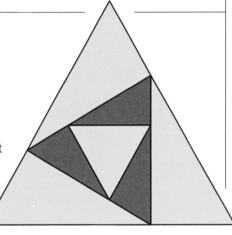

176 ★★☆☆☆

Fill in the grid so that each row, column, and region contains different digits 1 through 9. Note that each row and column contains less than nine digits.

4		3	7		1
	7			2	
1		9	4		
		7	8		5
	8			4	
9		5	6		7

177 ★★★☆☆

"Reforestation" has the apt anagram "A ton o' fir trees." The letters of the word are used to give a clue for the word itself. Find the word clued by each of the following apt anagrams.

Is abc's > _ _ _ _ _ _

A bar, etc. > _ _ _ _ _ _ _

i.e. Talon > _ _ _ _ _ _ _

Evade it! > _ _ _ _ _ _ _

Blah! Mess! > _ _ _ _ _ _ _ _

Deem as minor >
_ _ _ _ _ _ _ _ _ _

Go in, top star >
_ _ _ _ _ _ _ _ _ _

I call a miscount >
_ _ _ _ _ _ _ _ _ _ _ _

178 ★★★★☆

Divide the shape into five identical parts, cutting along the lines of the grid. Parts may be rotated or reflected.

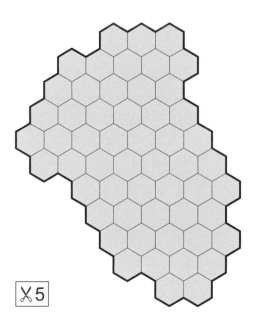

179 ★★☆☆☆

"Here we are at a square table, facing north, south, east, and west, and having the names North, South, East, and West. But none of us has a name that matches the direction we face," said the man facing north. "That's an interesting observation," Mr. East said, turning to his right. "Don't you agree, Mr. South?" Where is everyone sitting?

North

South

East

West

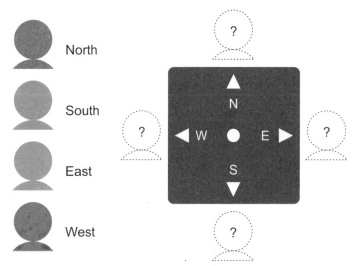

180 ★★★☆☆

Place the four chess pieces so that every piece attacks exactly four empty squares.

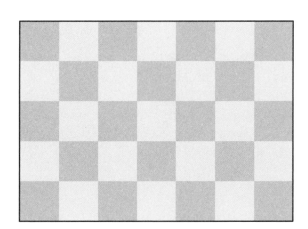

182 ★★★☆☆

How many squares of any size and orientation can you find in the shape? To count, the square must have four coins placed exactly at its respective corners.

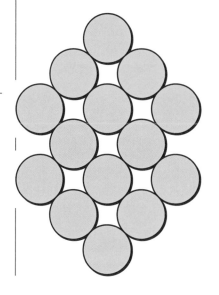

181 ★★☆☆☆

Put six distinct decimal digits into the boxes so that the equation is true.

$$\square^3 + \square^3 + \square^3 = \square^3 + \square^3 + \square^3$$

183 ★★★★☆ ✂2

Divide the shape into two identical parts, cutting along the lines of the grid. Parts may be rotated or reflected.

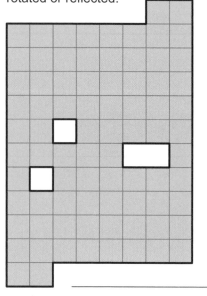

184 ★★★★☆

On the map below, the route ABCDEFGHA is an example of a cycle, a journey that ends at the starting point, without reusing any road. ABCDA, BCFGB, CDEFC, DEHAD, EFGHE, and GHABG is a set of these cycles that uses every road exactly twice, except for road DG, a new road. Find a set of cycles that uses each road exactly twice.

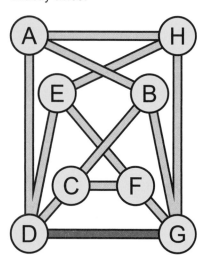

185 ★★★☆☆

Sara and her husband, along with three other couples, went on a sleigh ride Friday evening. With light flurries of snowflakes drifting down and cool crisp air, they snuggled down under the blanket provided while listening to the muted clip clop of the horses' hooves and the silent tinkling of the jingle bells on the harnesses. The sleigh ride took them to a big barn, where a dance was being held. Determine the full name of each couple and the title of the song each couple requested.

1. Brenda didn't request "Moonlight Serenade". The Grants didn't request "In the Mood".

2. Sara's husband wasn't Tom. Martha's husband wasn't Dave.

3. Mr. Patterson, who wasn't Dave, didn't request "Only the Lonely".

4. Michael, whose last name wasn't Grant, requested "Walking after Midnight".

5. Brian and his wife Kathy didn't request "Moonlight Serenade", which was requested by the Warners.

6. Tom Bradley didn't request "Only the Lonely". Martha's husband wasn't Michael.

Use the grid for help.

	Brenda	Kathy	Martha	Sara	Bradley	Grant	Patterson	Warner	"In the Mood"	"Moonlight Serenade"	"Only the Lonely"	"Walking after Midnight"
Brian												
Dave												
Michael												
Tom												
"In the Mood"												
"Moonlight Serenade"												
"Only the Lonely"												
"Walking after Midnight"												
Bradley												
Grant												
Patterson												
Warner												

Use the table for the solution.

First Name	First Name	Last Name	Dance Title

186 ★★★☆☆

Start in the center, and find a path that visits each hexagon exactly once. Your path can only turn gently (or go straight) in a yellow hexagon, and can only turn sharply (or go straight) in an orange hexagon.

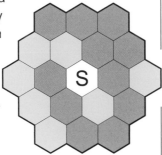

187 ★★☆☆☆

Place eight cards in a line to form a real 9-letter word. Cards can overlap each other but no card should be fully covered, rotated, or flipped.

Example:

188 ★★★☆☆

What seven letters should be placed in the blanks to create a meaningful sentence?

"It may not be _ _ _ _ _ _ _," said the headwaiter, "but I am _ _ _ _ _ _ _ to seat you, since we currently have _ _ _ _ _ _ _."

189 ★★★★☆

Fill in the grid so that each row, column, and stream contains different digits 1 through 7.

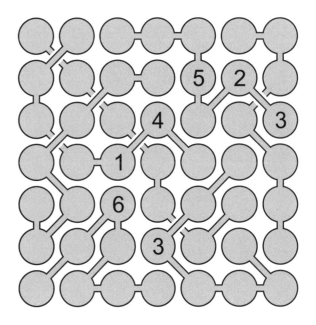

190 ★★★★☆

Nine matchsticks form three similar isosceles triangles. Move three matchsticks to form six similar triangles.

191 ★★☆☆☆

Swap two digits to restore the correct equation.

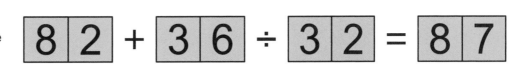

49

192 ★★★☆☆

Solve the maze using just the white paths and making right turns only. Left turns are strictly forbidden, even if there is no other choice.

193 ★★★★☆

Without lifting the pen from the paper, six lines can be drawn through the 4 x 4 grid of dots below, with the starting and ending points the same. How many circular arcs are necessary, in the same grid?

194 ★★☆☆☆

Fill in the grid so that each row, column, and region contains different digits 1 through 8. Note that some rows and columns contain less than eight digits.

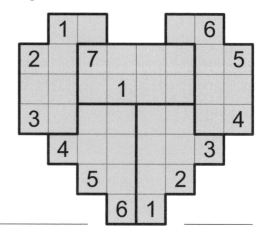

195 ★★★★★

Fill an 8 x 8 board with eight As, seven Bs, seven Cs, ..., seven Hs, and seven Is so that no two cells with the same letter are in a row, column, or 45-degree diagonal. Some cells already contain letters. Fill in the remaining cells.

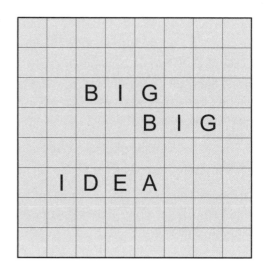

196 ★★★☆☆

What should replace the question mark?   C+7   F+4   P-6   S-9   H+?

197 ★★☆☆☆

Which man is
the odd one out?

198 ★★☆☆☆

Which of the four shapes cannot be formed
by using all five of the pieces on the right?
Pieces can be rotated, but not flipped over
or overlapped.

199 ★★★★☆

Divide the 6 x 6 board into groups of trominoes. These
can be I-trominoes, each with a dot at both ends, and
L-trominoes, each with a dot in the corner, as shown
to the left.

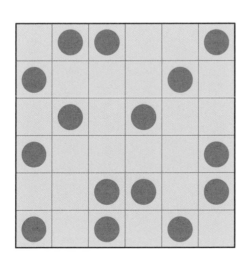

200 ★★☆☆☆

The series below follows its own logical
rules. What is the next number in the
series?

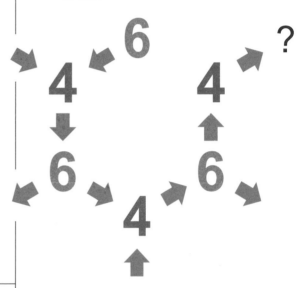

201 ★★★☆☆

In a triangular garden, 4 plants
are in a row. Add 6 more
plants to make 5 rows
of 4 plants. Each plant
must be in one of
the square plots.

202 ★★☆☆☆

Swap two digits to restore the correct equation.

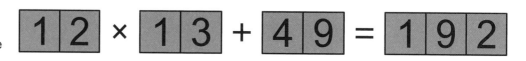

$$12 \times 13 + 49 = 192$$

203 ★★★☆☆

Four friends spent New Year's Eve together, reminiscing over the happenings in their lives over the year. They discovered that each of them had experienced something really good and something equally bad during the year. Determine the full name of each friend, the worst thing that happened to them, and the best thing that happened to them.

1. Mary didn't have a new baby. Larry didn't get a new job.

2. The four friends are represented by Ms. Lark, Mr. Marlin, the woman who got married, and the man who got laid off.

3. Ms. Philler's mom died but she didn't win the lottery. Fred didn't get laid off.

4. Fred didn't break up with his fiancée or get married.

5. Mr. Marlin got a new job.

6. Sally won the lottery. Mr. Singer didn't total his car.

	Lark	Marlin	Philler	Singer	broke up	car totaled	laid off	mom died	got married	new baby	new job	won the lottery
Fred												
Larry												
Mary												
Sally												
got married												
new baby												
new job												
won the lottery												
broke up												
car totaled												
laid off												
mom died												

Use the grid for help.

Use the table for the solution.

First Name	Last Name	Worst Thing	Best Thing

204 ★★☆☆☆

Find the only place in the grid where the word ONION can be spelled correctly. It might appear horizontally, vertically, backwards, or even diagonally, but the word is spelled out in a straight line.

	I	N	O	N	O	
I	N	O	I	N	I	N
O	O	I	N	O	O	I
I	N	O	O	I	N	O
N	I	O	I	N	O	N
N	O	N	I	O	O	I
	I	O	N	I	N	

205 ★★★☆☆

Divide the shape into seven identical parts, cutting along the lines of the grid. Parts may be rotated or reflected.

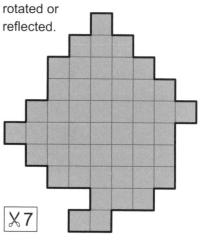

✂ 7

206 ★★★☆☆

Going along the lines of the grid, connect each pair of identical symbols with a single continuous line. Lines should cover all nodes of the shape, and cannot cross each other.

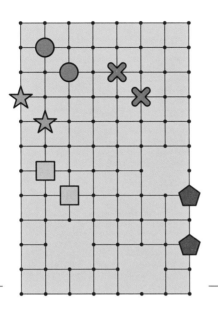

207 ★★★★★

Put the digits 1 through 9 in the weights so that each right side has torque exactly 1 more than the corresponding left side. Assume the rods and strings are weightless.

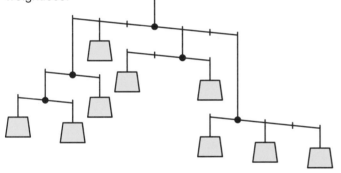

208 ★★☆☆☆

Which pattern A through E, when folded along the dotted lines, creates the same cube as the first pattern does?

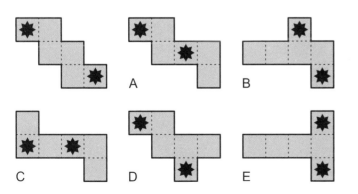

209 ★★☆☆☆

Enter the maze at the bottom, stepping over the red line, then step over a blue line, then a yellow line. Repeat the sequence (red, blue, yellow, red, blue, yellow...) until you can exit over the yellow line at the top. You must finish exactly red, blue, yellow.

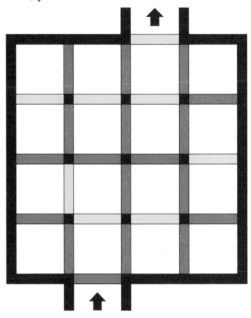

210 ★★★☆☆

Fill in the grid so that each row, column, and stream contains different digits 1 through 6.

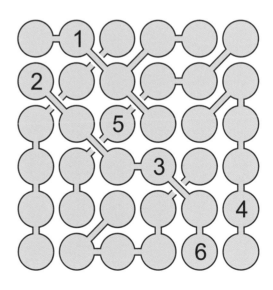

211 ★★★★★

Collect all the blue targets by rolling the red ball around the grid. The ball always rolls in a straight line until it hits a wall, and can therefore get trapped. What is the correct sequence of target pickups that allows all targets to be collected?

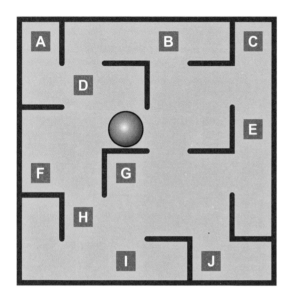

212 ★★☆☆☆

The office needs a new carpet. The carpet has been cut into L-shapes and T-shapes. Is it possible to put the carpet pieces down (without turning them over) so that none overlap, and without any being cut into smaller pieces? It is assumed that for the purpose of spreading the carpet, the nine computers are too large and cumbersome to move.

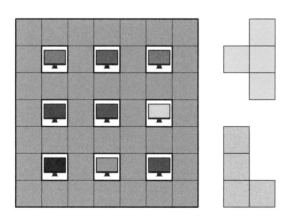

213 ★★☆☆☆

Place letters in the empty squares to get twelve words reading across and down.

214 ★★☆☆☆

What color should replace the question mark: red, brown, or green?

215 ★★★☆☆

Place a different positive digit in each box such that both equations are true, doing all calculations from left to right.

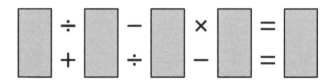

216 ★★★★☆

Divide the shape into three identical parts, cutting along the lines of the grid. Parts may be rotated or reflected.

✂3

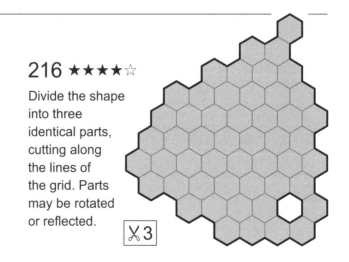

217 ★★★★☆

In the domino rectangle, trace a connected island of seven adjacent dominoes which contain two blank squares, two 1s, ..., two 5s, and two 6s.

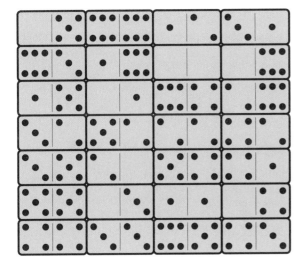

ALCHEMY
JARGONIZE
RINGLEADER
ENVIRONMENT
PUMPERNICKEL
PROCRASTINATING

218 ★★☆☆☆

What word is the odd one out?

219 ★★☆☆☆

Three of the four screws twisted into the wooden block are the same length. Which one differs? Note that all of the screws lie in one plane.

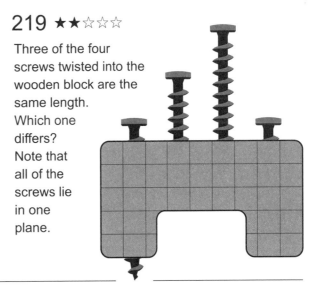

220 ★★☆☆☆

Place seven cards in a line to form a real 8-letter word. Cards can overlap each other but no card should be fully covered, rotated, or flipped.

Example:

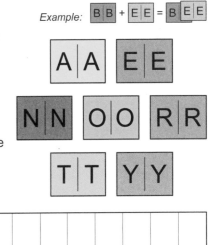

221 ★★★★☆

Fill in the grid so that each row, column, and region contains different digits 1 through 8. Note that some rows and columns contain less than eight digits.

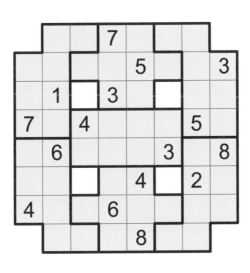

222 ★★☆☆☆

Fill each blank with a 2- or 3-letter word that will make two new words, each sharing the middle one.

SET _____ START

TAKE _____ FIELD

SHIP _____ SON

DESK _____ COAT

223 ★★☆☆☆

The poet, Robert Frost, had a pragmatic view of what we call home. To reveal the hidden quotation, place the letters into the grid. The letters above each column of the grid are the scrambled letters for that column only. The quotation reads horizontally, from left to right, across each row. The white squares indicate missing letters, the solid squares indicate the end of a word or the space between two words. Words can wrap around from one row to the next. Note that punctuation is omitted.

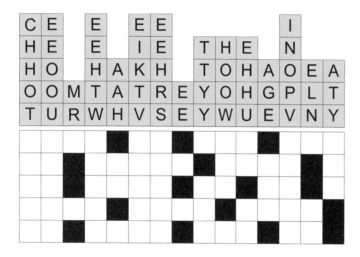

224 ★★☆☆☆

Decode the eight famous proverbs. All words longer than three letters are reduced to their first letter only.

W not, W not
C K the cat
An A a day K the D A
He who L L, L L
The B T in L are F
The P of the P is in the E
D put all Y E in one B
You win S, you L S

225 ★★★☆☆

The 12 matchsticks shown make one square and four triangles. Move the matches so that they make three squares and eight triangles.

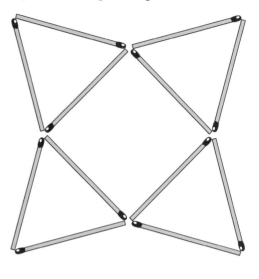

226 ★★☆☆☆

How many times can the chevron shape be found in the big hexagon pattern in any possible orientation (even mirrored)?

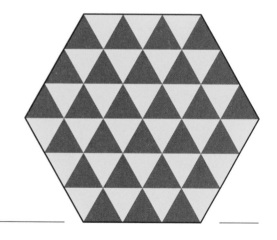

227 ★★★☆☆

Place the digits 1 through 9 in boxes to make both equations true. The larger of two neighboring digits is located higher.

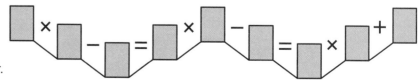

228 ★★★★☆

The square is assembled of the eight planks with holes. Rearrange planks into another square so that all twelve holes are only on its periphery.
You can rotate pieces but not overlap.

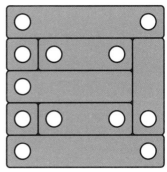

229 ★★★★☆

What is the smallest number m (in decimal), with digits ABCDEF...N (A ≠ 0) for which there is no pair of digits a, b (a ≠ 0) such that aABCDEF...Nb is a prime? Example: Try 97. Then for a = 1 and b = 3, we find that 1973 is a prime; so 97 is not such a number. On the other hand, 21267133 is such a number.

230 ★★★☆☆

Fill in the grid so that each row, column, and stream contains different digits 1 through 6.

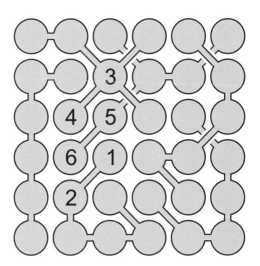

231 ★★★★★

The puzzle is quite like a crossword puzzle, with clues across and down. The difference is that the clues are about numbers, and the blank squares are filled with digits.

Each of the capital letters stands for a different positive integer (which may have many digits) represented in decimal. No numbers are allowed to have leading zeroes; this implies that a zero digit may not fill a space with a letter in it. Each blank square is to contain a single digit. Thus, for example, "a across" will be an eleven-digit integer.

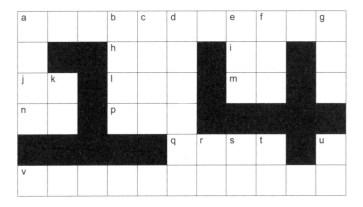

Across:
a. $V! + (B^{(V-L)})/B$
h. $B * W$
i. $V + E/A$
j. $G + D$
l. $S * R - B * W$
m. $B * (U - N - S + B * L)$
n. $B + G$
p. $R/B + A * V + S * (B * V + S)$
q. $S + A * R + U * W + (P + B)/A$
v. $A^{(X + F - S)}$

Down:
a. $D + B^L$
b. $R + Y * (V + S)$
c. $B * A * H$
d. $B * W + E * U + B * (L + B - (Y + B * L)/G)^N$
e. X^B
f. $B * P$
g. $B * W - S$
k. $V - B + D * B * (L - B) - (L + B) * (N + B)$
r. $P - E - B * (L + V + B - N * D) + (F * T + B * N * N)/N$
s. $E/A + L - U$
t. $S + T$
u. $B * W - X * X - U + S$

232 ★★★★☆

A rectangular sheet of paper is given a single fold as shown, with the result that at least two of the three triangles formed (A, B, or C) have an area which is an integer number of square inches.

Puzzle 1. What are the dimensions of such a sheet of paper with the smallest possible (nonzero) area?

Puzzle 2. Same problem only now we require m and n to also be integers.

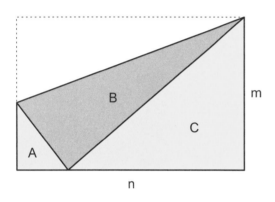

233 ★★☆☆☆

Redwolf   Silvercat
Goldfox   Whitehawk
Grayhorse

Ed saw these names over animal living areas 1 to 5. Curiously, none of the colors or animals matched the actual animal, or even a nearby animal. None of the names described another animal.

"My little joke," explained the owner.

Ed shook his head. "I'm glad Goldfox isn't a horse." Can you determine the color and type of each animal?

#	Name	Color	Type
1	Redwolf		
2	Silvercat		
3	Goldfox		
4	Whitehawk		
5	Grayhorse		

234 ★★★★☆

The shape consisting of thirteen equal balls is inscribed into a sphere. The inner ball is surrounded by twelve balls and it touches each of them. This shape is the other of the two tightest packings of thirteen balls in a sphere of the minimal radius. The shape can be split into three flat layers, as shown. Now, there are several puzzles.

Puzzle A. How many straight lines of three balls can you count in the shape?

Puzzle B. How many equilateral triangles of any size and orientation can you spot in the shape? To count, an equilateral triangle must have three balls whose centers lie exactly at its three corners.

Puzzle C. How many squares of any size and orientation can you spot in the shape? To count, a square must have four balls whose centers lie exactly at its four corners.

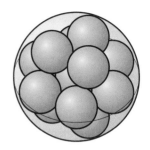

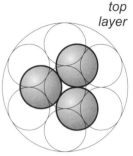

top layer

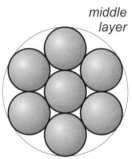

middle layer

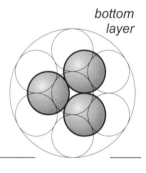

bottom layer

235 ★★★★☆

Program a robot with a list of movement commands (Up, Down, Left, and Right) to get it from Start to Finish. The robot moves one square at a time in the directions in its program. If the robot bumps into a wall, it performs the next possible move. When it runs out of instructions, it repeats the instructions it has in its cycle. The puzzle has a unique 6-command solution.

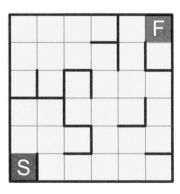

236 ★★☆☆☆

One of these letters, A, B, C, D, or E, is heavier than the other four. Which one is it?

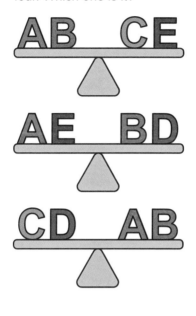

237 ★★☆☆☆

Travel the metro from your home station (K) to the market (C). Beware, all trains stop every second station only. For example, from K you can only exit or change at stations L and B.

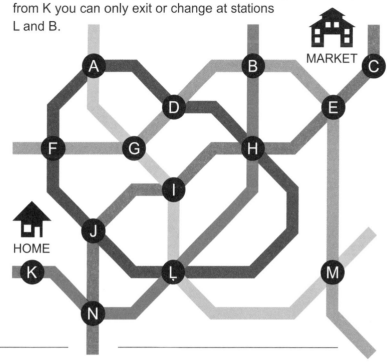

238 ★★☆☆☆

Swap two digits to restore the correct equation.

$$1 + 6 \times 6 \div 3 = 6 + 4$$

239 ★★★☆☆

Divide the shape into four identical parts, cutting along the lines of the grid. Parts may be rotated or reflected.

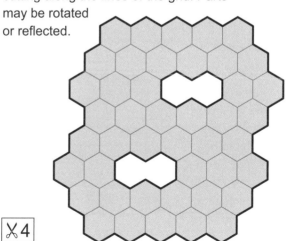

✂4

240 ★★☆☆☆

Fill in the grid so that each row, column, and region contains different digits 1 through 7. Note that some rows and columns contain less than seven digits.

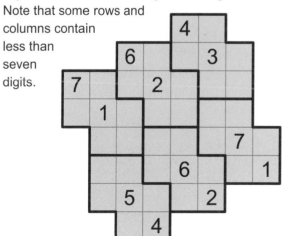

241 ★★★★☆

It's raspberry season! Tom and his friends were out walking in the woods when they discovered a whole hillside of wild raspberry bushes just loaded with ripe delicious raspberries. Tom raced back to his place to get some buckets for picking and all five of them spent the afternoon picking the luscious red berries. Determine each friend's full name, how many quarts of berries each picked, and what each one did with their berries.

1. Mr. Harding picked three quarts of raspberries during the afternoon. Fred's last name wasn't Richley and he didn't give his berries away to his neighbors.

2. Pete Waterby had two quarts more berries than the man who cooked them in muffins. Will's last name wasn't Dolby.

3. Will ate his berries with supper that night. Fred had more than one quart of berries.

4. The man who had four quarts of berries sold his to the local market.

5. Tom had more berries than Mr. Dolby but fewer berries than the one who froze his in the freezer for safekeeping.

6. Joshua didn't bring back the least amount of raspberries, which was one quart. Mr. Richley brought back five quarts, which was the largest amount brought back.

Use the grid for help.

Use the table for the solution.

	Dolby	Harding	Mann	Richley	Waterby	1 quart	2 quarts	3 quarts	4 quarts	5 quarts	ate them	cooked with them	froze them	gave them away	sold them
Fred															
Joshua															
Pete															
Tom															
Will															
ate them															
cooked with them															
froze them															
gave them away															
sold them															
1 quart															
2 quarts															
3 quarts															
4 quarts															
5 quarts															

First Name	Last Name	Quantity Picked	How Used

242 ★★★★☆

Six right prisms (with an equilateral triangle as their base) are flat and fully green. Using all these prisms, form a shape with the biggest possible cube with all six fully green faces. Find two substantially different solutions.

x6

243 ★★★★☆

Going through adjacent squares, find a path Start to Finish that passes through an equal number of squares of each (non-white) color. You may visit the white square. Visit no square more than once.

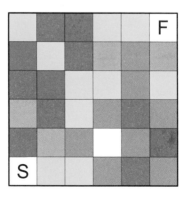

60

244 ★★★☆☆

Divide the shape into four identical parts, cutting along the lines of the grid. Parts may be rotated or reflected.

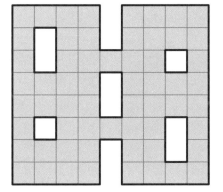

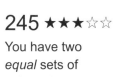

245 ★★★☆☆

You have two *equal* sets of colored hexagons. Nine hexagons partially overlap the other nine hexagons. Can you match identical hexagons in pairs?

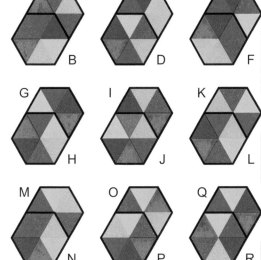

246 ★★☆☆☆

There is wisdom in doing some things yourself, rather than waiting for the professionals, as Murray Cohen points out in this quote. To reveal the hidden quotation, place the letters into the grid. The letters above each column of the grid are the scrambled letters for that column only. The quotation reads horizontally, from left to right, across each row. The white squares indicate missing letters, the solid squares indicate the end of a word or the space between two words. Words can wrap around from one row to the next. Note that punctuation is omitted.

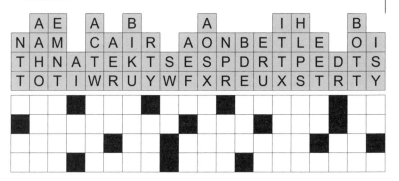

247 ★★☆☆☆

Place seven cards in a line to form a real 8-letter word. Cards can overlap each other but no card should be fully covered, rotated, or flipped.

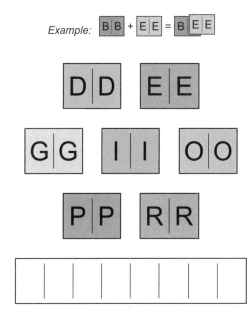

Example: B|B + E|E = B|E|E

248 ★★★☆☆

In the quilt below, find a small three-colored pattern which repeats exactly two times. Its diagram is shown next to the quilt. Note that these patterns can be rotated, but not overlapped and/or mirrored.

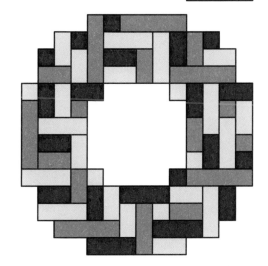

249 ★★★★★

In this chess puzzle, you are given only a list of all of the legal moves from a position. The problem is to find the current board position from which these moves arise. The notation for the moves is pretty standard. Each position can be reached by legal play starting from the usual opening position. White has six men, black has five. Black has no promoted men on the board. The legal moves are:

1. Rc1, 2. Bg3, 3. Rc2, 4. Pf6, 5. Rc3+, 6. Ph6, 7. Rc4, 8. Pf3, 9. Rc6, 10. Rc7, 11. Pxg6, 12. Rc8, 13. Kxe6. 14. Ra5, 15. Kxg8, 16. Rb5, 17. Bxg5, 18. Rd5, 19. Re5.

What is the position, and what is your estimate of the outcome of the game?

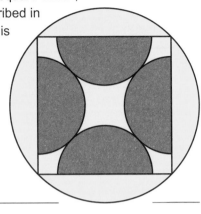

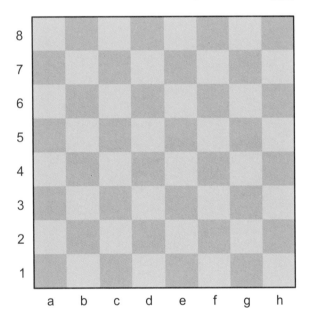

250 ★★☆☆☆

Exchange the position of the red and green pieces in the fewest number of moves/jumps. A piece moves into the nearest free spot or jumps over the neighboring piece into the free spot immediately behind that neighboring one. Red and green pieces move in turns.

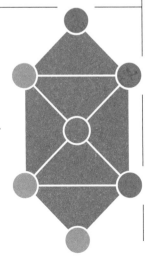

251 ★★★★☆

Four equal semicircles touch each other and are inscribed in a square which, in turn, is inscribed in a circle. What is the ratio between the total area of all four semicircles and the total light area?

252 ★★★☆☆

Place letters in the empty squares to get thirteen words reading across and down.

A		E		O		E		E	
C		M		L		T		V	
E		U		E		A		E	

253 ★★☆☆☆

Find two combinations of the same set of colors. The arrangement and sizes of the squares can be different.

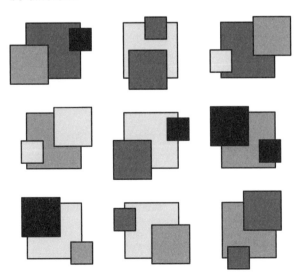

254 ★★★★☆

Starting from the central red atom, jump to any unvisited atom that matches either in shape or color (or both). Each jump must be straight along the grid's line, but may leap over other atoms in that line. Find a route that visits every atom once and once only.

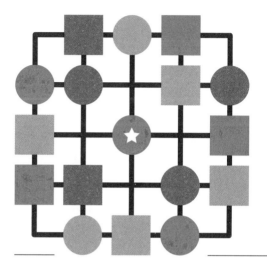

255 ★★★☆☆

Matchsticks are arranged into the shape of a mountain with a snowy peak. The shape contains one equilateral triangle.

   Puzzle 1. Move one matchstick to get two equilateral triangles.

   Puzzle 2. Starting from the initial position again, move two matchsticks to get three equilateral triangles. The moved matchstick from Puzzle 1 must not be moved now.

   Puzzle 3. Starting from the initial position again, move three matchsticks to get four equilateral triangles. The moved matchsticks from Puzzles 1 and 2 must not be moved now.

256 ★★★★☆

Put the digits 1 through 10 in the circles, using each number exactly once. The numbers outside the circles are either the sum of the numbers in all three of the nearest circles, or the sum of only two of them.

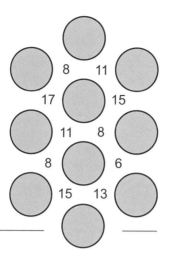

257 ★★★★☆

Puzzle 1. Divide three 4 x 3 rectangles into six different shapes, each with an area of six squares.

   Puzzle 2. Fit six shapes from the previous puzzle into the 6 x 6 board. You can rotate pieces and flip them over, but not overlap.

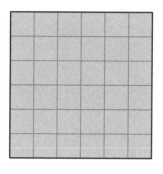

258 ★★★☆☆

Going along the lines of the grid, connect each pair of identical symbols with a single continuous line. Lines should cover all nodes of the shape.

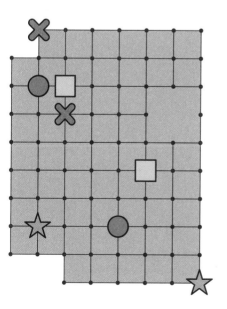

63

259 ★★★★☆

Fill in the grid so that each row, column, and stream contains different digits 1 through 7.

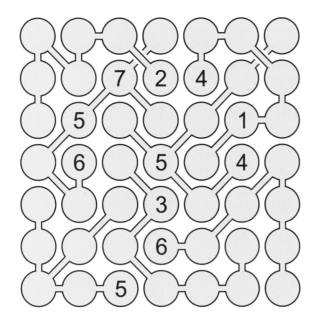

260 ★★★☆☆

What 2-syllable words starting with L, M, N, O, and P all rhyme with one another?

261 ★★★☆☆

Which pattern A through F, when folded along the dotted lines, creates the cube?

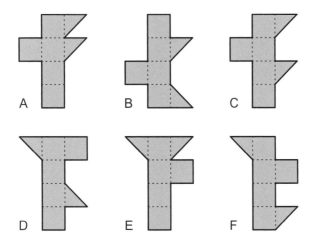

262 ★★★☆☆

Nob Yoshigahara noticed the curious property of the equation below. Are there any other numbers with this property?

$$12^2 + 33^2 = 1233$$

263 ★★★☆☆

The same letters in this calculation stand for the same digits, 0 through 9. Replace all letters with the digits so that the calculation is correct.

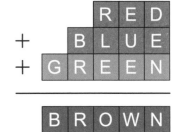

264 ★★★★☆

Connect the dots below into a collection of triangles. The triangles should not overlap or touch, and each triangle should contain one vertex of each color.

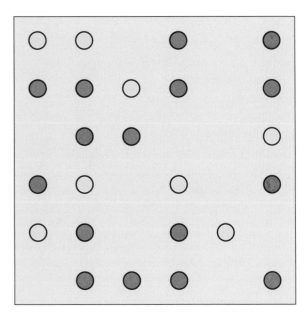

265 ★★★★★

Here is a reverse crossword. Using all the given clues and appropriate words from the word list, draw the proper 12 x 12 crossword layout.

Word list:

ACT	CHAT	LAMBS	OVER	SP.
AD	CHIT	LAMPS	PANTS	STOP
ART	CONCERN	L.C.	PIE	TO
AT	CONCERT	LEAD	PIG	TOP
BAR	COP	LEAK	PIN	TOPICAL
BEAD	DEAD	LEAP	RD	WANTS
BELT	DEFILED	MAN	RIDE	WE
B.O.	DEFINED	MAP	RISE	WHIM
BOAT	DEN	MARCH	RITE	WORD
BOLES	DEW	MATCH	SH.	WORK
BONES	EL	MOP	SHOP	YOUTH
BOXES	FEW	MOUTH	SI	
BY	HE	NO	SOP	

Clues across:

1. Near
2. A person may be inclined to walk carefully in this
3. One might expect a valet to attend to his employer's _____
6. That man
7. Lowercase (abbr.)
9. A good reporter won't ignore this
11. Brian Osborn (initials)
12. Pertaining to a subject
13. Not very useful if not suitable
15. Above
17. The kind of ball you would not expect to bounce
19. Yes (Spanish)
20. Road (abbr.)
21. In the direction of
22. One should be in good condition to engage in this
25. You and I
27. Water craft
28. Share (abbr.)
29. A woman may expect her _____ to draw compliments
30. A lawyer will _____ a phrase in a contract to his client's benefit
31. Generally appreciated when it is good

Clues down:

1. Encircling leather strip
2. One nation may take up arms if it feels its boundaries are being _____ by another
4. Negative
5. A motorist may hate to _____ to replace a faulty tire
8. May require wide patronage to be a success
9. These may be found on a farm
10. Elevated railway
11. Archaeologists may be delighted to come across these in their diggings
14. It may require a lot of feed to satisfy a hungry _____
16. A long _____ may prove tiresome
18. Public notice
22. It may be difficult to _____ an expedition into unknown territory
23. By
24. Among friends, this would not lead to an argument
25. Caprice
26. Not many
27. The court
28. Spanish (abbr.)

---

266 ★★★★☆

What is the longest sentence with all of its letters placed in reverse alphabetical order? Same letter can be used several times. For example:

ZOO FEE

267 ★★★☆☆

Find the pair of identical squares. They may be rotated.

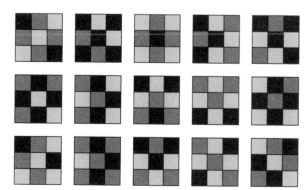

268 ★★★★☆

Fill in the grid so that each row, column, and region contains different digits 1 through 8. Note some rows and columns contain less than 8 digits.

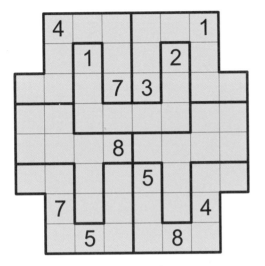

269 ★★★☆☆

Put the letters provided in the squares to spell two words that have very similar meanings. Linked squares will contain the same letter.

CEINRST

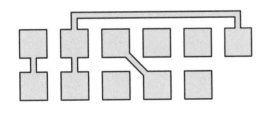

270 ★★★☆☆

Which two tiles create a perfect square with the full black square on it? Tiles can be rotated, but not flipped or overlapped.

271 ★★★★☆

Go from the top arrow to the bottom one through the pipes without jumping over the gaps.

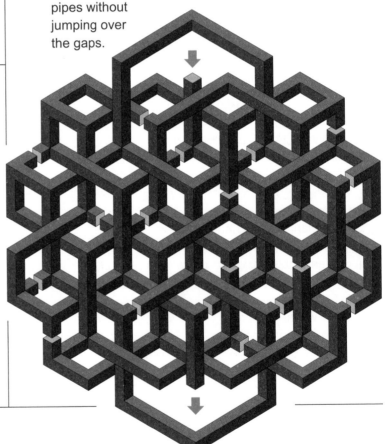

272 ★★★★☆

On a worn, 39-cm ruler, the only marks remaining are at 0, 8, 15, 17, 20, 21, 31, and 39. What is the shortest distance (in a whole number of centimeters) that cannot be measured between 2 marks?

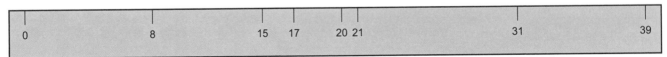

273 ★★★★☆

Following the grid lines, cut the shape into eleven equally sized pieces with four cuts. The pieces can have any shape. The cuts start on the periphery of the shape. None of them cross themselves, and each crosses the other cuts exactly once.

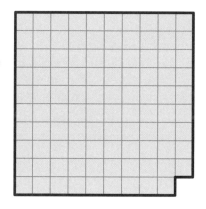

274 ★★★☆☆

How many triangles of any possible size and orientation can you find in the shape?

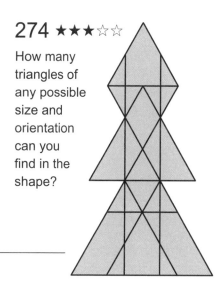

275 ★★★★☆

Five women studied their gardens last weekend, deciding it was high time the garden was cleaned out and new seeds were planted. So, each woman spent Sunday afternoon cleaning out her garden in preparation for planting. Each decided that during the week, they'd plant the first of the flowers planned for the garden. Determine the full name of each woman, what type of flower each was adding to the garden, and what day of the week each planted the seeds.

1. Ms. Smith didn't plant her flowers on Wednesday. Harriet Peach didn't plant roses.

2. Betty planted mums, but not on Tuesday. Harriet planted her flowers before Martha, but after Gertrude. The irises were planted on Friday but not by Sara.

3. Sara, whose last name wasn't Wells, didn't plant her flowers on Thursday. Betty's last name wasn't Smith.

4. The roses were planted on Wednesday. The daffodils were planted on Tuesday.

5. Ms. Mann didn't plant her flowers on Friday or Monday. Martha's last name wasn't Smith.

6. The five women were represented by Ms. Fiddler, the woman who planted irises, the woman who planted flowers on Thursday, the woman who planted tulips, and Harriet.

Use the grid for help.

Use the table for the solution.

	Fiddler	Mann	Peach	Smith	Wells	daffodils	irises	mums	roses	tulips	Monday	Tuesday	Wednesday	Thursday	Friday
Betty															
Gertrude															
Harriet															
Martha															
Sara															
Monday															
Tuesday															
Wednesday															
Thursday															
Friday															
daffodils															
irises															
mums															
roses															
tulips															

First Name	Last Name	Planted Flower	Day of the Week

276 ★★★★★

Substitute digits for the letters so as to make a "correct" division statement in decimal arithmetic. The same numerical digit must be substituted for each occurrence of a given letter, and no digit may be used for two different letters. The leading (leftmost) digit of each number formed cannot be zero. Each box is just a place holder and may have any but must have some digit placed within. Hint: U = 0.

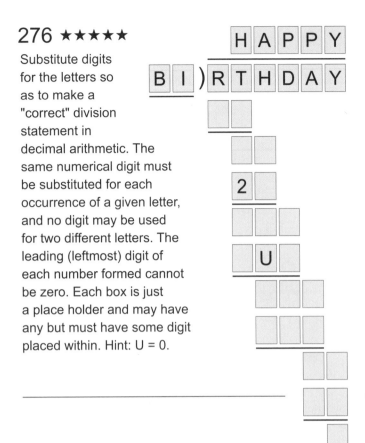

277 ★★★☆☆

There are many theories on what makes a great marriage, but is there really a formula for successful life between two individuals? Here is Dave Meurer's thoughts on the subject. To reveal the hidden quotation, place the letters into the grid. The letters above each column of the grid are the scrambled letters for that column only. The quotation reads horizontally, from left to right, across each row. The white squares indicate missing letters, the solid squares indicate the end of a word or the space between two words. Words can wrap around from one row to the next.

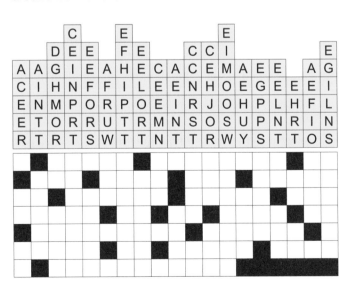

278 ★★★★☆

Fill each box with the digits 2, 4, 6, or 8 so that each equation is true.

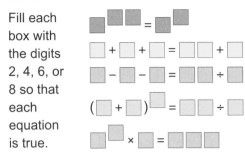

279 ★★☆☆☆

Start at the mountain's foot and get to its top. Always move from one face to adjacent one, and never jump over faces. Color faces on your climbing route must constantly repeat, in groups of three. For example, yellow-green-purple-, and then again, yellow-green-purple-, and so on up to the top.

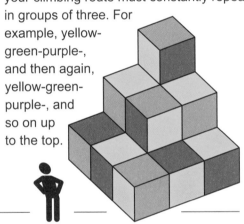

280 ★★★★☆

Put the digits 1 through 7 in the yellow weights, and do the same for the blue weights, so that the whole system balances. Assume the rods and strings are weightless.

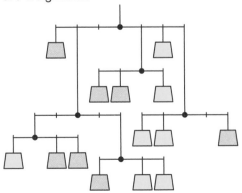

281 ★★★☆

Divide the Mytra shape with three matchsticks into:
1. Two parts of the same area.
2. Three parts of the same area.
3. Four parts of the same area.

Each matchstick is four cells long.

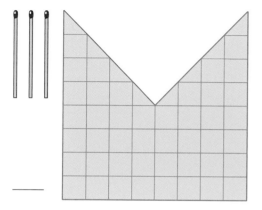

282 ★★★☆

Three identical cubes are hung in space as shown. On the bottom plane they make three different projections: square, rectangle, and right hexagon. Determine the ratio between the areas of the projections.

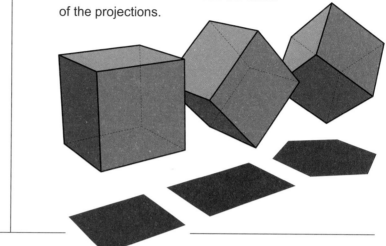

283 ★★★★☆

The letter triple "azz" occurs twice in razzmatazz. What words contain each of the following triples twice?

ach ama ant ard eno hua igh mat ono
osc own phi rac tic tin tor und utt

284 ★★★★☆

Place the twenty pieces (five of each color) into the grid so that no two pieces of the same color share an edge.

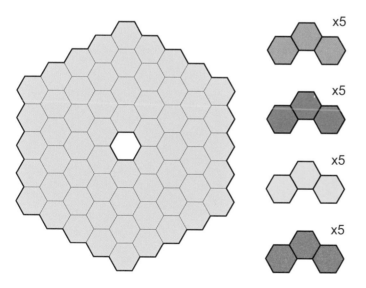

285 ★★★★☆

Cross all cells of the checkered T-shape shown below with a chain of four connected straight line segments (not necessarily closed in a loop) so that cells in the chain will go in the alternating manner: ...-b-w-b-w-... A cell is crossed if a line crosses any two of its sides no matter how it goes over a cell. No cell should be crossed twice, and no node of the shape can be crossed at all. Also, the chain of lines should not turn at a cell. At the same time lines can cross each other outside the shape. A small sample with two connected lines crossing in the alternate manner all cells of a 2x2 checkered square is shown.

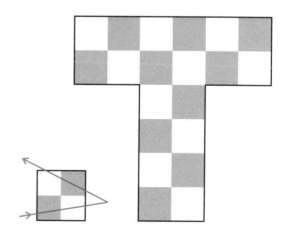

286 ★★☆☆☆

Starting from a cell of the grid and during each next step moving to a vertically, horizontally, or diagonally adjacent one, you can read some word(s). Note that you can pass any letter just once. For example, you can easily find the words "IN" or "OK" which are not the longest possible words hidden in the grid. Can you find two 5-letter words? Can you improve these results?

A	B	C	D
E	F	G	H
I	J	K	L
M	N	O	P

287 ★★★★☆

Divide the shape into four identical parts, cutting along the lines of the grid. Parts may be rotated or reflected.

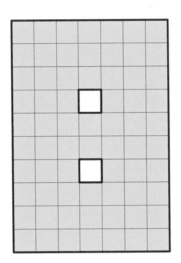

✂4

288 ★★★☆☆

Moving horizontally or vertically, get from dot to star. The number at the end of each row or column indicates how many steps you must take in that direction. You must step the full number and must stay on the grid, so if a number is too large look for an alternative.

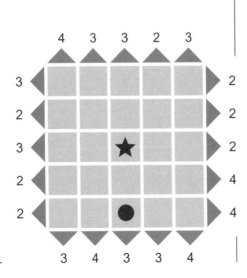

289 ★★★★★

You have one 8 1/2-by-12-inch sheet of paper and seven 3-by-5-inch cards. Cover as much of the paper as possible with the cards. They may overlap or extend off the sides of the paper, but no mutilation of the paper is permitted.

Puzzle 1. No cutting or folding of the cards allowed.

Puzzle 2. Cutting and folding of the cards is allowed, but any cut made must leave an uncut connection of at least 1/2 inch between sections of a card.

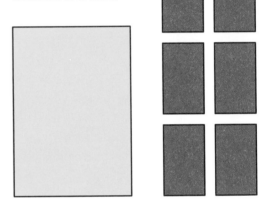

290 ★★★☆☆

Fill in the grid so that each row, column, and stream contains different digits 1 through 6.

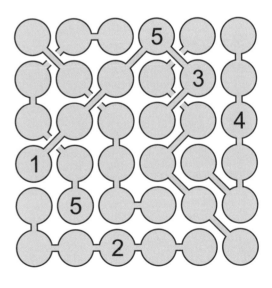

291 ★★★☆☆

Exchange the position of the red and blue counters in the fewest number of moves. A counter moves into the nearest free spot, but it can not jump over the wall or other counter.

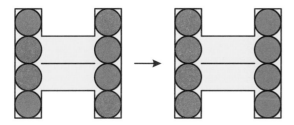

292 ★★★★★

You have seven balls which look exactly the same. Four balls weigh 3 units each, while the remaining three ones weigh 4 units each. Using only a pair of scales, in four weighings split the balls into two groups containing just balls of the same weight each. Is it possible to achieve the goal in three weighings?

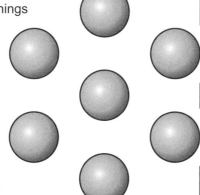

293 ★★★☆☆

Place rook, bishop, and knight on the chess board so that every piece (including the placed king and queen) attacks an equal number of empty squares.

294 ★★★☆☆

One word is written in light on the dark tiles, while the other is in dark on the light ones. Then each light letter on the dark tiles was overlapped with the dark letter from the light tile immediately below it. And vice versa—each dark letter on the light tiles was overlapped with the light letter from the dark tile immediately above it. Reveal these two words—their meanings are related.

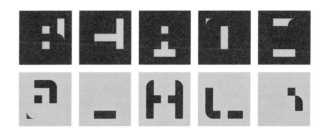

The shapes of the letters are shown below.

295 ★★☆☆☆

In the inlay, which shape exactly similar to one of those shown on the left (bird, arrow, or fir) can be found? The shape can differ in size and orientation, but its outline must be full and uninterrupted.

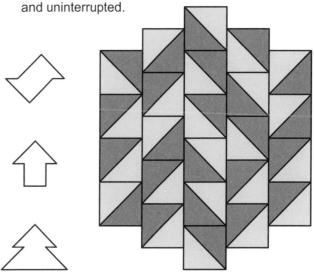

296 ★★★★☆

Place the thirteen given letters into the grid so that a chess king could move one square at a time to trace out each of the seven given words.

A A
H I
I K
L M
M N
O U W

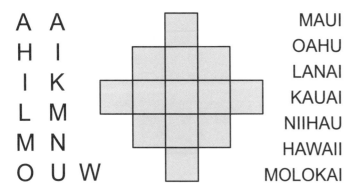

MAUI
OAHU
LANAI
KAUAI
NIIHAU
HAWAII
MOLOKAI

297 ★★★★☆

In the binary number system all positive integral powers of two have numerical representations which contain all the binary digits (namely 0 and 1). Example: $10^{10} = 100$. In the decimal system this is, of course, not true. For example: $2^{77} = 151,115,727,451,828,646,838,272$ fails to contain the digits 0 and 9.

What is the smallest positive integral power of two whose decimal representation contains all the digits 0 through 9?

298 ★★★☆☆

Insert the digits 0 through 9 into the circles to make the five equations true when read from left to right. Each digit is used exactly once.

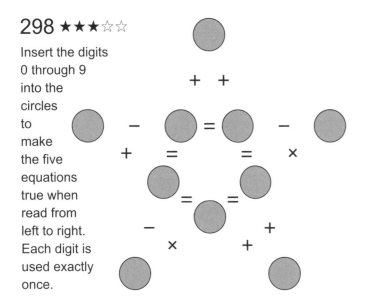

299 ★★★☆☆

You have six buildings of rectangular forms and a vacant city block of 6 x 7, as shown in the illustration. Put all buildings into the block to make an occupied city block. The buildings can be rotated, but they cannot touch each other even at a corner. How many different variations of the occupied city block can you find?

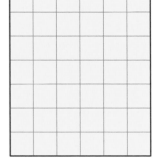

300 ★★★☆☆

Divide the shape into five identical parts, cutting along the lines of the grid. Parts may be rotated or reflected.

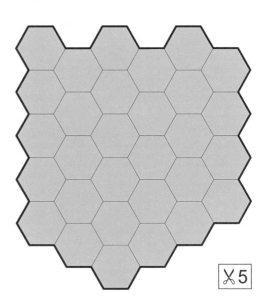

✂5

72

Solutions

1

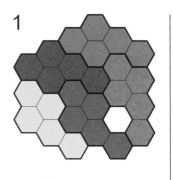

2

3

4

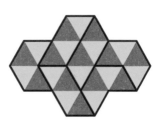

5

ALUMINUM	COPPER
ARSENIC	GOLD
HYDROGEN	CALCIUM
IODINE	SULFUR
IRON	LEAD
NICKEL	PHOSPHORUS

6

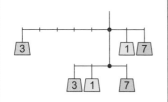

7

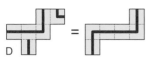

8

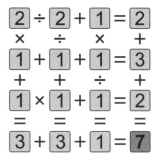

14

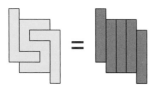

9

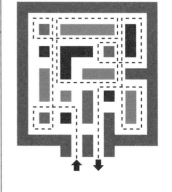

10

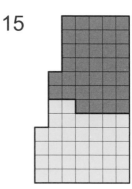

11

Al spent 5 coins, Bee spent 145 coins, Cal spent 55 coins, Dot spent 115 coins, Ed spent 95 coins.

13

EAST OR WEST - HOME IS BEST

12

Puzzle 1. There are 11 different dancers.

Puzzle 2. These 5 dancers can be spotted just once each.

Puzzle 3. The following dancer can be spotted three times.

15

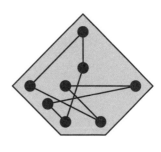

18

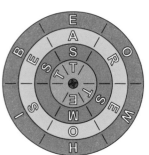

19

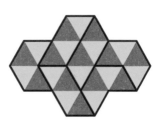

16

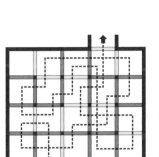

17

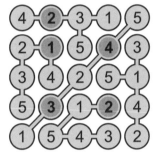

20

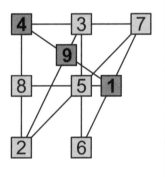

21

22

FALSE and TRUTH

23

24

27

The only position fitting the constraints is that shown below. After the move 0-0-0+ white has an easy win.

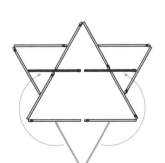

26

First Name	Last Name	Water Sport	Afternoon Activity
Cindy	White	canoeing	painting
Harry	Mann	swimming	archery
Mike	Smith	kayaking	pottery
Sara	Heart	sailing	tennis

32

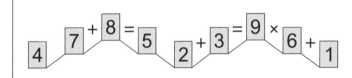

25

There are two solutions.

```
    8 6 9 0 5        8 6 9 0 5
+   1 6 4 0 5    +   1 6 7 0 5
+     3 7 1 0    +     3 4 1 0
+     2 3 1 0    +     2 3 1 0
  ───────────      ───────────
  1 0 9 3 3 0      1 0 9 3 3 0
```

28

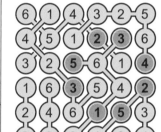

29

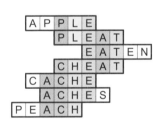

30

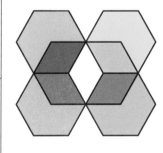

31

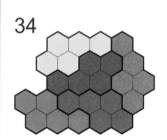

34

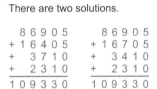

33

37

First Name	Last Name	Summer Job	College Major
Michael	Rain	waiter	Business
Paul	Spring	janitor	Finance
Sam	Winter	landscaper	Engineering
Walt	Cloud	technician	Teaching

44

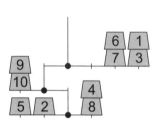

48

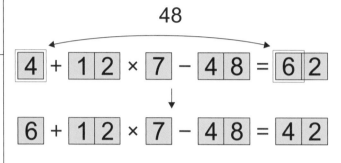

45

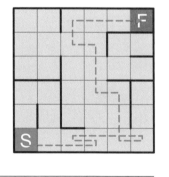

35

Puzzle 1. The earliest solution occurs after 861.1 miles, at which time the readings are 13206.7 and 984.5. There is only one other solution, when all distinct digits occur, namely, 0.9 mile later at 13207.6 and 985.4.

Puzzle 2. The following strategy will produce all distinct digits after the least driving: Harry should drive 0.1 mile, then reset the right-hand dial to 888.8. Now after only 1.8 additional miles the dials will read: 12347.5 and 890.6.

38

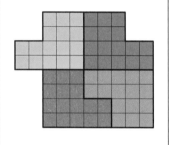

41

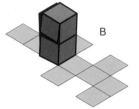

47

Program: R R R L U U

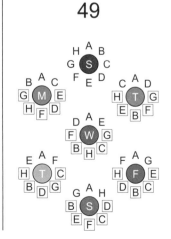

39

I'm 43 years old.

36

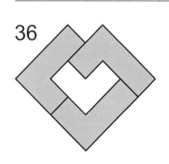

40

B-C-D-A

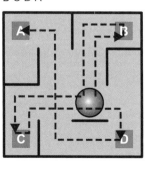

42

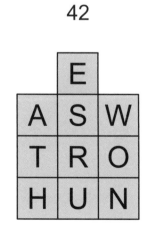

43

The 4th piece – it has a smaller area, while the other four pieces have equal area.

49

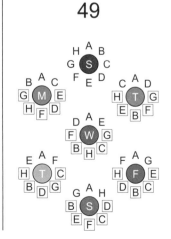

50

51

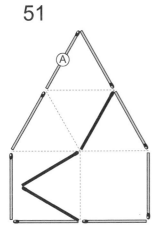

56

One of possible 32-move tours is shown. Additionally, it has the minimum possible path length.

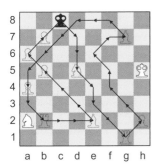

57

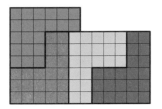

46

53

4 apples can be distributed in 35 ways among 4 people.

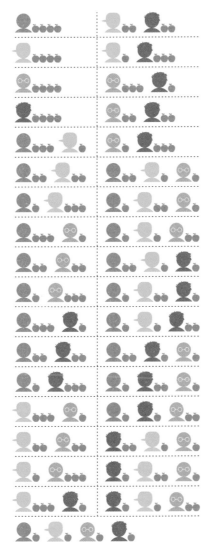

52

Pentagon N has no twin.

54

65

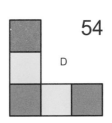

58

59

B - the visible areas of blue and yellow faces are always equal.

60

3	2	**4**	5	1	6
6	3	5	1	**2**	4
1	6	2	4	5	**3**
5	4	1	3	6	2
2	**5**	3	6	4	1
4	1	6	2	3	5

61

55

The red piece is not used to build the square shape.

63

First Name	Last Name	Relationship	Home City
George	Smith	Dan's brother	Chicago
Natalie	Green	Janet's sister	New York
Robert	West	Dan's uncle	Providence
Sara	Mann	Janet's cousin	Boston

70

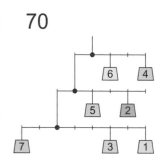

62

There are four groups of digits of the decimal position(s) in numbers from 1 to 5000—the ones, tens, hundreds, and thousands—represented by 1 through 9 and 0 with adding "hundred" and "thousand" for the two latter groups. Note that a "zero" is never used in word representations of the numbers.

In the ones: 1, 2, and 6 use 3 letters; 4, 5, and 9 use 4 letters; 3, 7, and 8 use 5 letters.

In the tens: 10 uses 3 letters; 40, 50, and 60 use 5 letters; 20, 30, 80, and 90 use 6 letters; 70 uses 7 letters.

There is a specific sub-group of "teens." In them: 11 and 12 use 6 letters; 15 and 16 use 7 letters; 13, 14, 18, and 19 use 8 letters; 17 uses 9 letters.

In the hundreds: 1, 2, and 6 use 3 plus 7 letters; 4, 5, and 9 use 4 plus 7 letters; 3, 7, and 8 use 5 plus 7 letters.

In the thousands (remember that we only have integers from 1 to 5000): 1 and 2 use 3 plus 8 letters; 4 and 5 use 4 plus 8 letters; 3 uses 5 plus 8 letters.

From the teens 17 looks promising, since it has no immediate counterparts in the tens, teens, and units. But 41, 42, 46, 51, 52, 56, 61, 62, and 66 also use 9 letters. So 17 (and any combinations with it) is not unique.

The only possibility left is 3 thousand, whose letter representation uses 14 characters. So the unique class is "14" with 3000 as a single number in it.

64

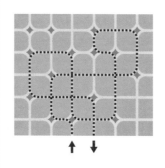

66

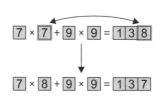

67

Areas of the bubbles:
Red = $\pi 2.5^2 + \pi 0.5^2 = 6.5\pi$;
Blue = $\pi 2^2 + \pi 1.5^2 + \pi 0.5^2 + \pi 0.5^2 = 6.75\pi$;
Yellow = $\pi 1.5^2 + \pi 1.5^2 + \pi 1.5^2 = 6.75\pi$.

Thus, the red bubbles cover the least area.

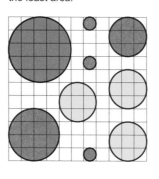

68

In the pattern, the wire shape can be found in all possible orientations 16 times.

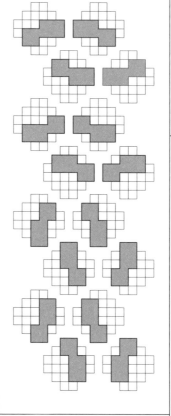

69

71

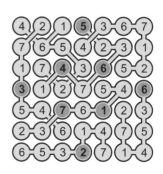

72

The dande**LIONS** are plentiful in the front yard this year!

"We w**ANT EATER**s!" exclaimed the organizer of the County Fair Pie Contest.

In Ja**PAN**, **THER**e are many different holidays.

In Jap**AN**, **T**here are many different holidays.

"Please **JACK**, **AL**low me," said the chauffeur, opening the door for his employer.

Amy g**OT TER**rific grades on her report card this semester!

"See that mark you ma**DE**? **ER**ase it, right now!" ordered the teacher.

74

First Name	Last Name	Flavored Teas	Snacks
Lindsay	Manor	green tea	apple crisp
Martin	Tanner	Russian caravan tea	peanut butter fudge
Sheila	Croupe	peppermint tea	chocolate chip cookies
Travis	Walker	orange pekoe tea	cinnamon rolls

73

QuICK BroWN FoX JuMPS oVer THe LAZY DoG. The blanks here consist of all the letters appearing only once in this well-known sentence.

79

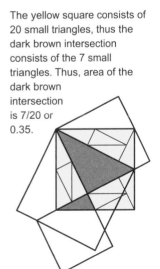

75

5 chairs is the maximum.

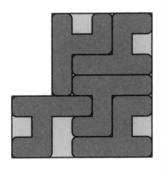

78

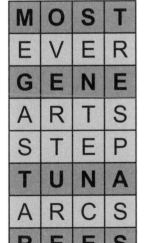

76

$25 + 64 = 89$

77

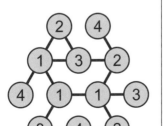

82

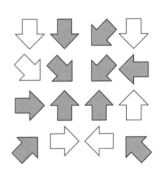

80

The matrix shows all possible combinations of dark and light quarters in all possible orientations with the increment of 45 degrees. The thirtieth disc is the only missing combination among 30 possible ones.

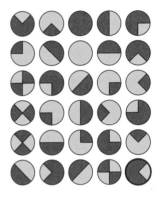

81

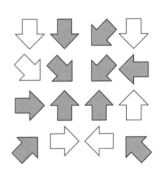

88

The yellow square consists of 20 small triangles, thus the dark brown intersection consists of the 7 small triangles. Thus, area of the dark brown intersection is 7/20 or 0.35.

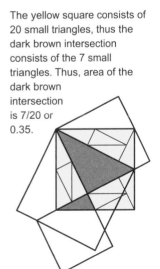

83

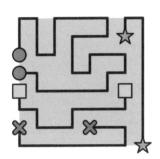

85

86

There are 50 coin isosceles triangles of all sizes and orientations.

 x5

 x5
 x5

 x5
 x5

 x5
 x5

 x5
 x10

84

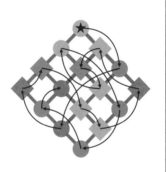

87

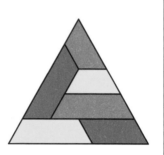

89

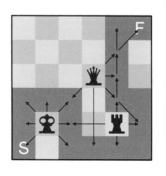

92

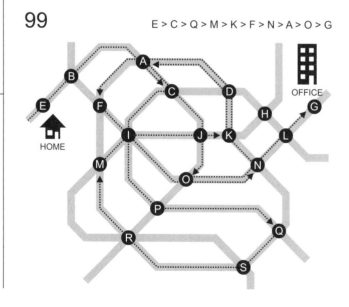

90

40 – if the next shape is: (a) a square - add 1; (b) a circle - multiply by 2; (c) blue - subtract 4 (in addition to the normal square or circle function).

 4 8 9 14 15 12 24 21 22 40

93

First Name	Last Name	Item Won	Amount Paid
Abigail	Smart	gold necklace	$50
Mark	Parson	music box	$100
Sally	Welsh	Victorian lamp	$75
Tom	Vialle	antique clock	$25

91

Block 1 = block 4; block 2 = = block 3. Thus, the total volume of the light blocks is the same as the total volume of the dark blocks.

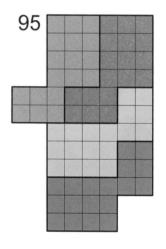

95

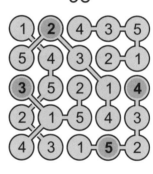

94

Each vowel can be changed to any other vowel to produce a word: BALL > BELL > BILL > BOLL > BULL; LEST > LIST > LOST > LUST > LAST; MISS > MOSS > MUSS > MASS > MESS; POT > PUT > PAT > PET > PIT; TUN > TAN > TEN > TIN > TON.

96

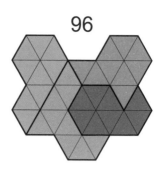

97

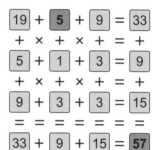

98

19 + **5** + 9 = 33
+ × + × + = +
5 + 1 + 3 = 9
+ × + × + = +
9 + 3 + 3 = 15
= = = = = = =
33 + 9 + 15 = **57**

99

E > C > Q > M > K > F > N > A > O > G

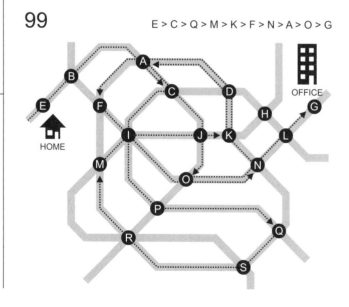

104

$$1\;2\;+\;1\;2\;\times\;1\;3\;=\;1\;5\;7$$

$$1\;3\;+\;1\;2\;\times\;1\;2\;=\;1\;5\;7$$

105

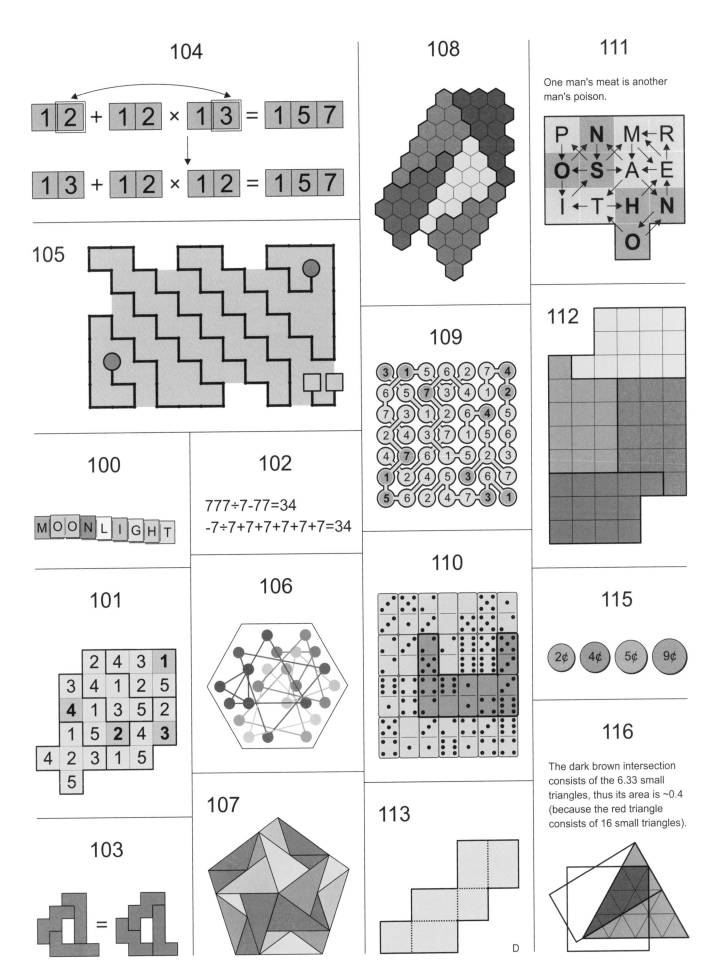

108

111

One man's meat is another man's poison.

100

MOONLIGHT

102

777÷7-77=34
-7÷7+7+7+7+7=34

109

101

2	4	3	**1**	
3	4	1	2	5
4	1	3	5	2
1	5	**2**	4	**3**
4	2	3	1	5
5				

106

110

112

115

2¢   4¢   5¢   9¢

116

The dark brown intersection consists of the 6.33 small triangles, thus its area is ~0.4 (because the red triangle consists of 16 small triangles).

107

113

D

103

=

114

First Name	Last Name	Activity	Color
Samantha	Wilson	underwater swim	green
Sara	Grimes	water balloon toss	blue
Sheila	Norton	croquet	purple
Sherry	Sanford	water relay	black

124

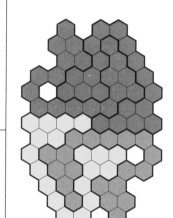

130

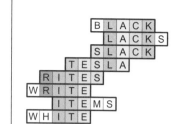

117

In the grid, there are 52 squares of two sizes.

x38   x14

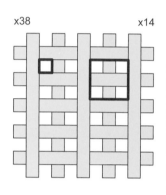

118

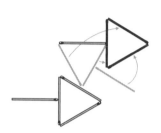

131

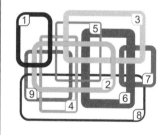

120

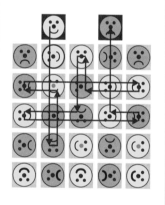

125

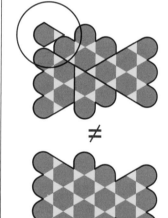

≠

119

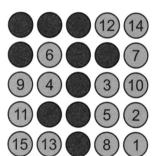

121

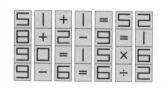

133

123

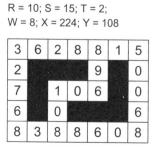

122

The only two solutions are 3108456729 and 3180456729.

126

R = 10; S = 15; T = 2;
W = 8; X = 224; Y = 108

3	6	2	8	8	1	5
2				9		0
7		1	0	6		0
6		0				6
8	3	8	8	6	0	8

134

127

There are two instances of the same double letter, JJ and WW

ABCDEFGHIJKLMNOPQRSTUVWXYZ
SRQPONMLKJIHGFEDCBAZYXWVUT

128

First Name	Last Name	Fish Size	Fish Type
Charlie	Warner	52 pounds	bluegill
George	Blue	49 pounds	trout
Norm	Harmon	48 pounds	flounder
Sam	Remane	50 pounds	bass

129

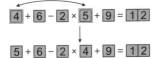

$4 + 6 - 2 × 5 + 9 = 12$

$5 + 6 - 2 × 4 + 9 = 12$

135

$7 + 1 = 8$
$-$ $×$ $÷$
$1 + 3 = 4$
$=$ $=$ $=$
$6 ÷ 3 = 2$

136

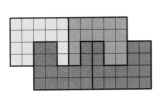

HASTE
MAKES
WASTE

137

Numbers show each third step, after which you must change color.

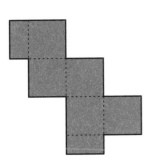

138

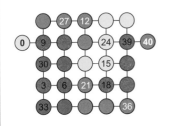

139

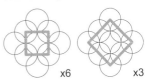

140

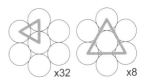

B

132

Puzzle A. There are 6 straight, 3-ball lines in the shape. They all go through its center and contain the inner ball as their middle one.

x6

Puzzle B. There are 40 equilateral triangles of all sizes and orientations, as shown.

x32   x8

Puzzle C. There are 9 squares of all sizes and orientations, as shown.

x6   x3

Puzzle D. It is obvious that the radius of a ball {r} is three times smaller than the radius of the sphere {R}. Hence, the volume of the ball $\{V_r=(4/3)\pi r^3\}$ is 27 times smaller than the volume of the sphere $\{V_R=(4/3)\pi R^3\}$. Thus, the ratio between the total volume of all the thirteen balls and the sphere is 13 : 27.

r

R

141

39 needs 3 steps:
3 x 9 = 27
2 x 7 = 14
1 x 4 = 4
    77 needs 4 steps:
7 x 7 = 49
4 x 9 = 36
3 x 6 = 18
1 x 8 = 8

142

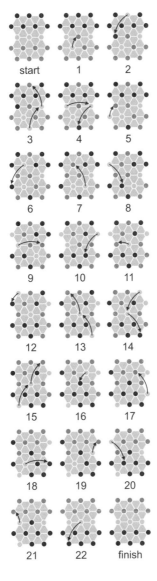

start   1   2
3   4   5
6   7   8
9   10   11
12   13   14
15   16   17
18   19   20
21   22   finish

149

JELLYFISH

143

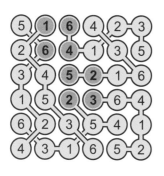

144

Easy: 13, 17, and 79.
   Moderate: 149, 157, 167, 179, 347, 359, and 389.
   Hard: 1237, 1249, 1259, 1279, 1789, 3467, and 3469.
   Hardest: 12689, 13457, 13469, 13789, 15679, and 34589.

To solve the above challenges a computational aid of some sort to do part of the work can be helpful. But all these primes with not more than five digits can be located in a table of primes within about twenty minutes. In this case it becomes rather a sort of a visual puzzle.

148

Block 2 + block 3 = block 5; block 1 + block 4 > block 6. Thus, the total volume of the dark blocks is greater than the total volume of the light blocks.

145

146

DON'T FOUL YOUR OWN NEST.

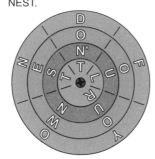

147

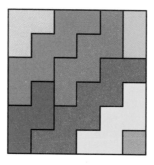

150

153

Last Name	Pet Name	Pet Type	Order Visited
Ford	Cutie	parrot	4th
O'Henry	Toby	dog	1st
Smith	Nobs	horse	3rd
Walker	Puck	cat	2nd

151

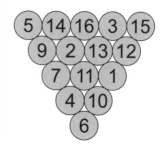

152

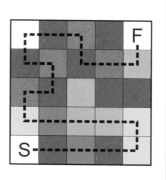

154

GOLD	TIN	MERCURY

ZINC	LEAD	PHOSPHORUS

159

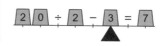

155

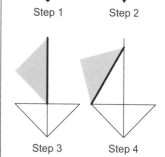

156

163

12:40pm = Twenty-to-One

157

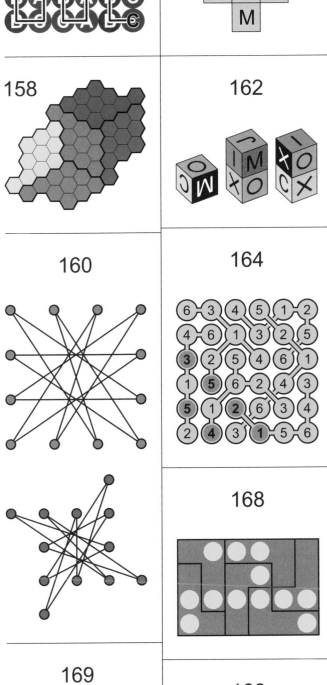

158

160

161

162

164

168

169

ACE FILM NOR TUX
Solution improved by Harry Nelson.

166

170

Child's Name	Favorite Food	Forgotten Item	Ice Cream
Barry	peanut butter cookies	bread	mocha almond
Cindy	blueberries	roast beef	coffee
Peter	graham crackers	paper towels	strawberry
Rose	chocolate bar	carrots	vanilla

173

165

167

172

7−8	8÷4	4=5			
4=5	3−2	7−8	8÷4		
4=5	7−8	9+4	3−2	8÷4	
4=5	7−8	9+4	3×3	8÷4	3−2

171

174

The 2nd cube—each of the other cubes has proportion of its total yellow and red surface areas 1 : 1.

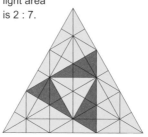

175

The big triangle consists of 54 small, right-angled triangles: 12 dark and 42 light. Thus, the ratio between the total area of all the dark parts and the total light area is 2 : 7.

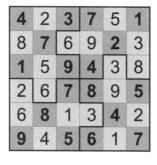

176

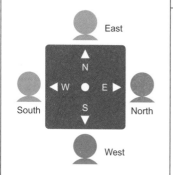

4	2	3	7	5	1
8	7	6	9	2	3
1	5	9	4	3	8
2	6	7	8	9	5
6	8	1	3	4	2
9	4	5	6	1	7

177

Is abc's > <u>basics</u>
A bar, etc. > <u>cabaret</u>
i.e. Talon > <u>toenail</u>
Evade it! > <u>deviate</u>
Blah! Mess! > <u>shambles</u>
Deem as minor > <u>misdemeanor</u>
Go in, top star > <u>protagonist</u>
I call a miscount > <u>miscalculation</u>

178

179

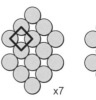

East
South
North
West

180

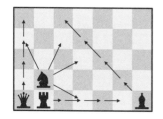

186

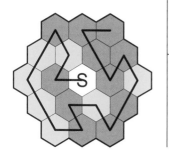

187

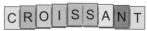

181

$$0^3 + 7^3 + 8^3 = 1^3 + 5^3 + 9^3$$

182

There are 15 coin squares of all sizes and orientations.

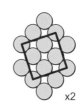

x7   x4   x2   x2

185

First Name	First Name	Last Name	Dance Title
Brian	Kathy	Grant	"Only the Lonely"
Dave	Sara	Warner	"Moonlight Serenade"
Michael	Brenda	Patterson	"Walking after Midnight"
Tom	Martha	Bradley	"In the Mood"

183

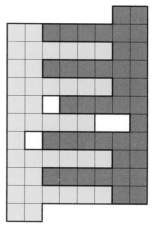

184

DGHED   DCFED

ABGHA   DABCFGD

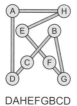

DAHEFGBCD

188

The three blanks could be filled with the same 7 letters, in the same order: "It may not be NOTABLE," said the headwaiter, "but I am NOT ABLE to seat you, since we currently have NO TABLE."

189

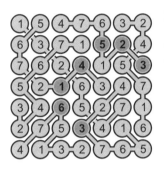

190

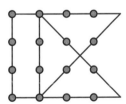

193

six straight lines

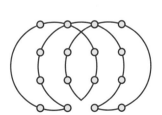

three circular arcs

191

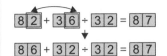

192

194

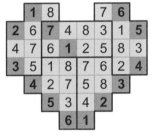

196

Each pair in the sequence stands for the position of letter J in the English alphabet. So, as shown above, C + 7 positions = F + 4 positions = P - 6 positions = S - 9 positions = J. Thus, the correct answer is H + 2.

A_1 B_2 C_3 D_4 E_5

F_6 G_7 H_8 I_9 J_{10}

K_{11} L_{12} M_{13} N_{14} O_{15}

P_{16} Q_{17} R_{18} S_{19} T_{20}

U_{21} V_{22} W_{23} X_{24} Y_{25}

Z_{26}

195

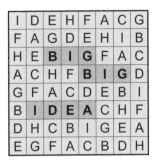

197

The 3rd man—it consists of 15 small triangles, while all others consist of 16.

198

199

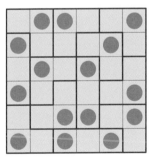

202

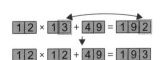

200

4—all arrows next to a number change it into the next one in the series. Add 2 for each arrow pointing AT the number and subtract 2 for each arrow pointing AWAY from the number.

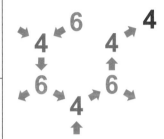

201

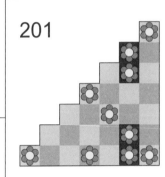

204

205

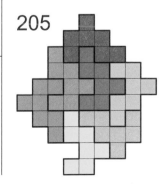

203

First Name	Last Name	Worst Thing	Best Thing
Fred	Marlin	totaled car	new job
Larry	Singer	laid off	new baby
Mary	Philler	mom died	got married
Sally	Lark	broke up	won the lottery

206

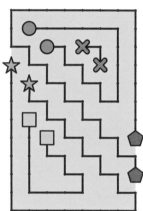

207

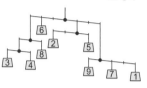

208

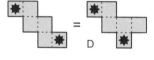

211

D > A > F > B > H > J > G >
I > E > C

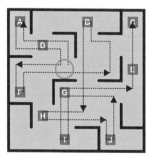

209

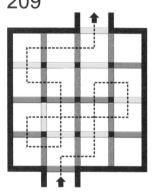

210

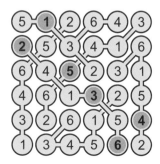

212

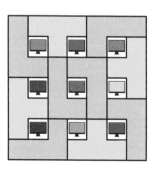

213

214

The green color should replace the question mark—intersection of the yellow and blue color filters.

215

216

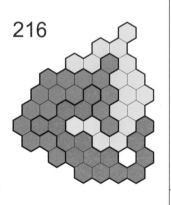

222

SET <u>UP</u> START

TAKE <u>OUT</u> FIELD

SHIP <u>PER</u> SON

DESK <u>TOP</u> COAT

217

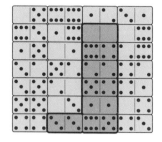

218

Each word but ALCHEMY contains the name of an element:

alchemy

j<u>ARGON</u>ize

ring<u>LEAD</u>er

env<u>IRON</u>ment

pumper<u>NICKEL</u>

procras<u>TIN</u>ating

219

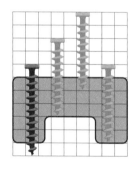

225

Rearrange the matchsticks into a 3-D octahedron; it contains 3 squares and 8 triangles.

223

H	O	M	E		I	S		T	H	E		P	L	A
C	E		W	H	E	R	E		W	H	E	N		Y
O	U		H	A	V	E		T	O		G	O		T
H	E	R	E		T	H	E	Y		H	A	V	E	
T	O		T	A	K	E		Y	O	U		I	N	

231

A = 4, B = 2, D = 7,
E = 116, F = 6,
G = 89, H = 1001,
L = 13, N = 5,
P = 118, R = 1000,
S = 1, T = 10, U = 3,
V = 14, W = 100,
X = 12, Y = 419.

8	7	1	7	8	2	9	1	2	0	1
1			2	0	0		4	3		9
9	6		8	0	0		4	6		9
9	1		5	8	5					
						4	3	3	1	5
1	7	1	7	9	8	6	9	1	8	4

220

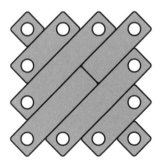

A T T O R N E Y

224

Waste not, want not

Curiosity killed the cat

An apple a day keeps the doctor away

He who laughs last, laughs longest

The best things in life are free

The proof of the pudding is in the eating

Don't put all your eggs in one basket

You win some, you lose some

229

The answer is 2437.

221

	4	8	7	2	1	6	
6	2	1	4	5	8	7	3
5	1		3	6		8	4
7	3	4	8	1	6	5	2
1	6	5	2	7	3	4	8
3	7		5	4		2	6
4	8	7	6	3	2	1	5
	5	2	1	8	7	3	

232

Puzzle 1. The smallest possible area of a rectangular sheet of paper with at least two of the three triangles (A, B, or C) having an area of an integer number of square inches can be reached with n = 2.028877 and m = 1.595004. The total area of the sheet is 3.236068 square inches. Area A = .236068; area B = 1; and area C = 1 square inches.

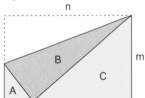

Puzzle 2. The smallest solution is as shown. The sheet has sizes n = 10 and m = 8. Area A = 6; area B = 25; and area C = 24 square inches. The total area of the sheet in the case its sizes also are integers makes 80 square inches, which is almost 25 times bigger than in Puzzle 1.

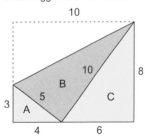

233

#	Name	Color	Type
1	Redwolf	gold	hawk
2	Silvercat	white	horse
3	Goldfox	gray	wolf
4	Whitehawk	red	cat
5	Grayhorse	silver	fox

234

Puzzle A. There are 3 straight, 3-ball lines in the shape. They all go through its center and contain the inner ball as their middle one.

 x3

Puzzle B. There are 34 equilateral triangles of all sizes and orientations, as shown.

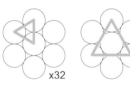 x32   x2

Puzzle C. There are 6 squares of all sizes and orientations, as shown. x6

226

There are 19 small hexagons in the big hexagon shape. Each hexagon contains 6 chevrons. Thus, there are 114 chevrons in the big hexagon shape.

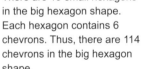

227

$5 \times 4 - 1 = 3 \times 9 - 8 = 2 \times 6 + 7$

228

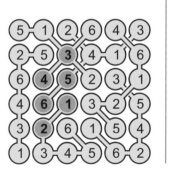

230

238

$1 + 6 \times 6 \div 3 = 6 + 4$

$1 + 6 \times 6 \div 6 = 3 + 4$

236

A + B = C + E and
C + D = A + B show
that E = D. Then,
A + E = B + D gives A = B.
Since A = B and D = E, only
C can be heaviest alone.

240

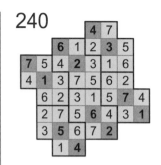

235

Program: U R D L R U

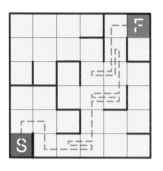

243

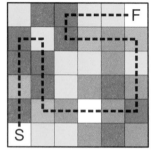

237

K > B > M > A > H > C

239

250

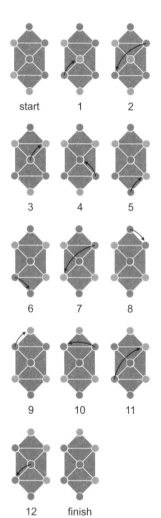

242

Two substantially different
solutions to the puzzle are
shown in the diagrams. In
both cases within each shape
you have a small cube with all
of its six faces fully green. A
cube's edge is as long as a
prism's thickness.

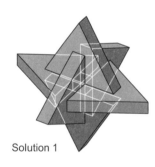

Solution 1

Solution 2

241

First Name	Last Name	Quantity Picked	How Used
Fred	Dolby	2 quarts	cooked with them
Joshua	Richley	5 quarts	froze them
Pete	Waterby	4 quarts	sold them
Tom	Harding	3 quarts	gave them away
Will	Mann	1 quart	ate them

246

252

245

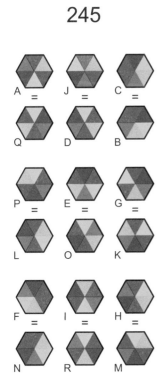

A = Q
J = D
C = B
P = L
E = O
G = K
F = N
I = R
H = M

247

P O R R I D G E

251

It is obvious that the radius of each small semicircle {r} is two times smaller than the radius of the big circle {R}. Hence, the area of the four semicircles $\{4 \times 0.5\pi r^2 = 2\pi r^2\}$ makes a half of the big circle's area $\{\pi R^2 = \pi(2r)^2 = 4\pi r^2\}$. Thus, the ratio between the total area of all four semicircles and the total light area is 1 : 1.

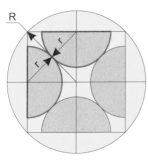

248

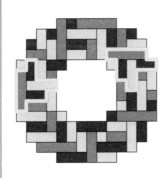

249

The only position fitting the constraints is that shown. In the puzzle, it is necessary that black's previous move was Pg5 by a pawn formerly on g7, thus allowing an en-passant capture on this move. Since Pg5 is not a very "good" move, it may be argued that perhaps black will not fare as well as the position suggests in the rest of the game, though normally white would lose no matter what move is made here.

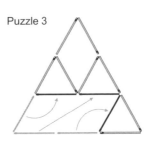

253

244

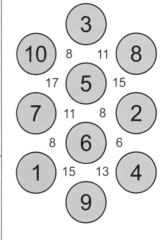

254

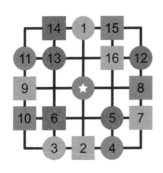

255

Puzzle 1

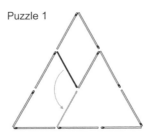

Puzzle 2

Puzzle 3

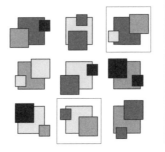

256

257

Puzzle 1

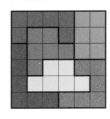

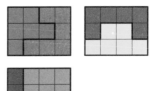

Puzzle 2

258

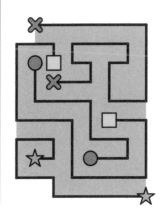

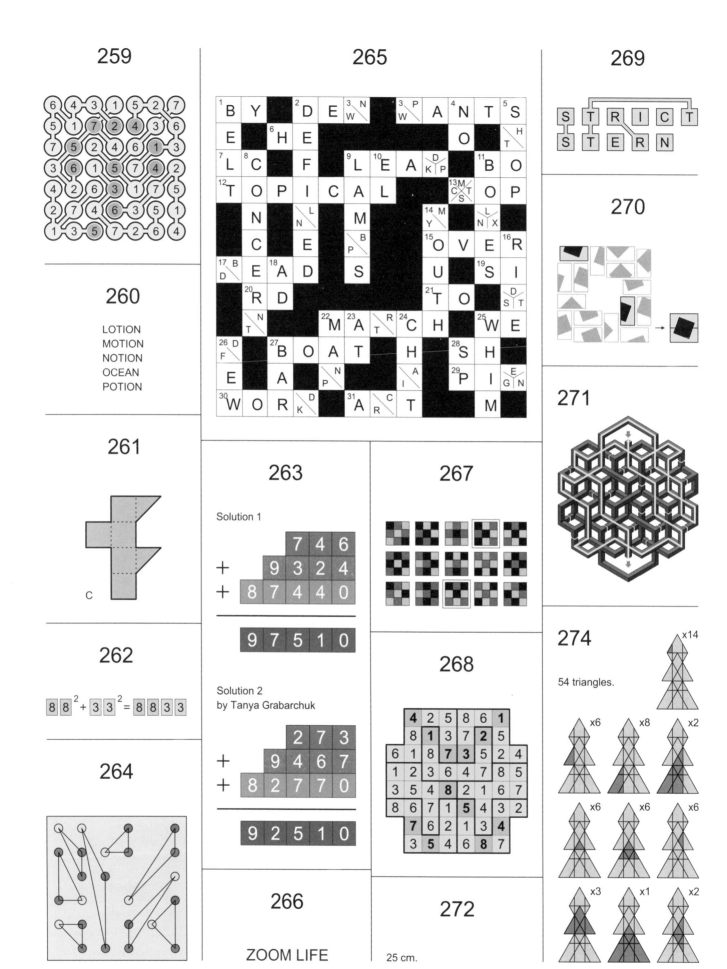

259

260

LOTION
MOTION
NOTION
OCEAN
POTION

261

C

262

$88^2 + 33^2 = 88 33$

264

263

Solution 1

```
    7 4 6
+   9 3 2 4
+ 8 7 4 4 0
---------
9 7 5 1 0
```

Solution 2
by Tanya Grabarchuk

```
    2 7 3
+   9 4 6 7
+ 8 2 7 7 0
---------
9 2 5 1 0
```

265

266

ZOOM LIFE

267

268

269

STRICT
STERN

270

271

272

25 cm.

274

54 triangles.

x14

x6   x8   x2

x6   x6   x6

x3   x1   x2

275

First Name	Last Name	Planted Flower	Day of the Week
Betty	Mann	mums	Thursday
Gertrude	Smith	tulips	Monday
Harriet	Peach	daffodils	Tuesday
Martha	Wells	irises	Friday
Sara	Fiddler	roses	Wednesday

277

A | | G | R | E | A | T | | M | A | R | R | I | A | G | E | | I | S
| N | O | T | | W | H | E | N | | T | H | E | | P | E | R | F | E
C | T | | C | O | U | P | L | E | | C | O | M | E | S | | T | O | G
E | T | H | E | R | | I | T | | I | S | | W | H | E | N | | A | N
| I | M | P | E | R | F | E | C | T | | C | O | U | P | L | E | | L
E | A | R | N | S | | T | O | | E | N | J | O | Y | | T | H | E | I
R | | D | I | F | F | E | R | E | N | C | E | S

273

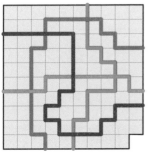

276

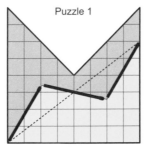

281

Puzzle 1

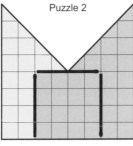

Puzzle 2

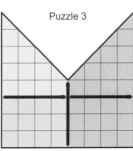

Puzzle 3

278

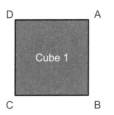

$2 \; 24 = 8 \; 8$

$8 + 8 + 8 = 22 + 2$

$8 - 2 - 2 = 24 \div 6$

$(2 + 2)^2 = 64 \div 4$

$6^2 \times 8 = 288$

279

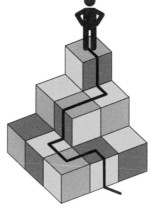

280

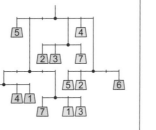

284

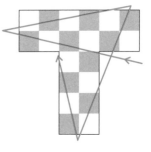

282

AB = AD = 1;
S_{Cube1} = AB * AD = 1 * 1 = 1.
EF = 1;
EH = sqrt($1^2 + 1^2$) = sqrt2 = 1.414;
S_{Cube2} = EF * EH = 1.414.
JN = sqrt($1^2 + 1^2$) = sqrt2 = 1.414;
KN = 2JK;
$JN^2 + JK^2 = KN^2$;
$JN^2 + JK^2 = 4JK^2$;
$JN^2 = 3JK^2$;
$JN^2 = (sqrt2)^2 = 2$;
$JK^2 = 2/3$;
JK = sqrt(2/3) = 0.816;
S_{Cube3} = 3 * (JK * JN / 2) = 3/2 * 1.414 * 0.816 = 1.732;
Thus, $S_{Cube1} : S_{Cube2} : S_{cube3}$ = 1 : 1.414 : 1.732.

Cube 1

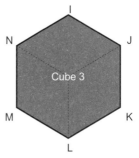

Cube 2

Cube 3

285

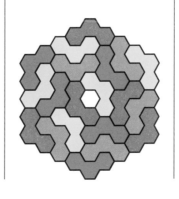

283

stomACHACHe,
AMAlgAMAted,
ANTioxidANT,
cARDboARD,
phENOmENOn,
ChiHUAHUA,
hIGHlIGHt,
MATheMATics,
mONOtONOus,
OSCillOSCope,
dOWNtOWN,
PHIlosoPHIcal,
RACetRACk,
anTIClimacTIC,
procrasTINaTINg
TORmenTOR,
UNDergroUND,
scUTTlebUTT.

287

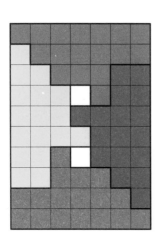

288

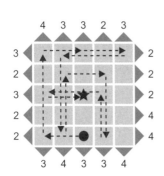

286

KNIFE

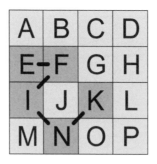

PLONK

290

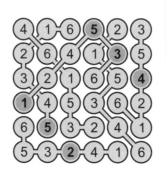

293

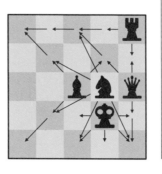

289

Puzzle 1. The best known covering, with only ~3.74 square inches not covered is shown in the diagram.

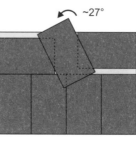

Puzzle 2. One way to cover the entire paper is shown below. First, place six cards, then cut and fold the seventh to obtain an exact covering, as shown

291

start 1 2
3 4 5
6 7 8
9 10 11
12 13 14
15 16 finish

294

WHITE and BLACK

295

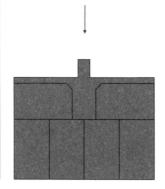

94

292

We have four lighter (L) and three heavier (H) balls, as shown in Fig. 1. Now take any three pairs of balls and compare them on the scale. We will have one of the following possibilities:

Case A. After three weighings we have the distribution of balls on the scales as shown in Fig. 2. And so we can determine just one heavier ball (H).

Case B. After three weighings we have the distribution of balls on the scales as shown in Fig. 3. And so we can determine just two lighter balls (L and L), and one heavier ball (H).

Case C. After three weighings we have the distribution of balls on the scales as shown in Fig. 4. And so now all balls' weights are determined.

Case D. After three weighings we have the distribution of balls on the scales as shown in Fig. 5. And so now all balls' weights are determined.

For Cases A and B we need to perform one more weighing. Take only two single balls from any two even pairs; balls must be from different even pairs—exactly one ball from each chosen even pair. Comparing these two balls on the scales, we will have one of the following possibilities:

Case A1, Fig. 6. Thus these balls (and their respective even pairs) are light (L and L) and balls in the third even pair are heavier (H and H). And so now all balls' weights are determined.

Case A2, Fig. 7. Thus these balls are one lighter (L) and the other heavier (H), and therefore their respective even pairs contain lighter and heavier balls, respectively. Balls in the third even pair are lighter (L and L). And so now all balls' weights are determined.

Case B1, Fig. 8. Thus these balls are one lighter (L) and the other heavier (H), and therefore their respective even pairs contain lighter and heavier balls, respectively. And so now all balls' weights are determined.

Fig. 1

Fig. 2

Fig. 3

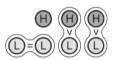

Fig. 4

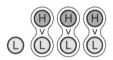

Fig. 5

Fig. 6

Fig. 7

Fig. 8

296

297

The smallest positive integral power of two whose decimal representation contains all the digits 0 through 9 is 2^{68} = 295,147,905,179,352,825,856

298

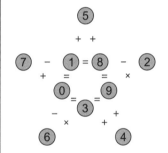

299

300

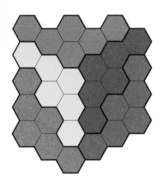

Index

Puzzle Types

Difficulty Levels